FLIGHI
SIMULATOR
ADVENTURES

FOR THE
MACINTOSH, AMIGA, AND ATARI ST

David Florance, Tom R. Halfhill, and Philip I. Nelson

COMPUTE!™ Publications,Inc. abc

Part of ABC Consumer Magazines, Inc.
One of the ABC Publishing Companies

Greensboro, North Carolina

COMPUTE! Publications, Inc., Post Office Box 5406, Greensboro, NC 27403, (919)
275-9809, is part of ABC Consumer Magazines, Inc., one of the ABC Publishing Companies, and is not associated with any manufacturer of personal computers. Amiga is
a trademark of Commodore-Amiga, Inc. Atari and Atari ST are trademarks of Atari
Corporation. Macintosh is a trademark licensed to Apple Computer, Inc.

Flight Simulator is produced by Microsoft Corporation and copyright 1984 and 1986
by Bruce A. Artwick. *Flight Simulator II* is produced by SubLOGIC Corporation and
copyright 1984 and 1986 by Bruce A. Artwick.

Contents

Preface
Flights of Fancy

Who among us can say that we've passed through childhood without ever pretending we were a bird or a plane? Probably no one.

The compulsion to fly has been part of human nature for centuries, and in an age of jumbo jets, space shuttles, hang gliders, pedal-powered flying wings of gossamer, and globe-girdling miracles of engineering like the tiny *Voyager*, it survives undiminished.

But even though flight is as widely accessible as the nearest airline ticket counter, something's missing. Everyone can fly, but not anyone can *fly*. It soon becomes apparent to the frequent commercial air traveler that the difference between riding a bus and flying on a jet airliner is mainly the level of altitude, not the level of exhilaration. Squinting out of a porthole-sized window just isn't the same as soaring on the winds under your own control.

You could take flying lessons, but it would cost several thousand dollars to qualify for a private pilot's license. And then you'd have to spend thousands more to buy or lease a plane.

You could enlist in an aviation branch of the armed forces—if you're a young, healthy person with 20/20 vision and the talent to compete against the best of your generation.

You could take up hang gliding—if you didn't mind risking a few broken bones, or worse.

At one time or another, the authors of this book have considered all of these options and more, and even pursued some of them. Unfortunately, the age of flight for everyman (and everywoman) has not quite arrived, although it's not too far distant.

Fortunately, the age of personal computing *has* arrived. Computers have found places in millions of homes. Grade-school children are learning to use computers even before they master the three R's. And there's scarcely a business in the country that hasn't either bought a computer or considered buying one.

With millions of personal computers installed in homes and offices, the stage was set a few years ago for the introduction of the first flight simulator program. It was a smashing success.

And why not? It appeals to those centuries-old fantasies, giving everyone with access to a computer the chance to fly.

Of course, some may object that it's not *really* flying. You don't even leave your chair. No matter how good the graphics may be, you're not soaring through the heavens—you're simply staring at the cathode-ray glow of a video screen.

True. But the undeniable success of the flight simulator doesn't derive from its deniable simulation of reality. Instead, its uncanny abilities to entertain our flights of fancy are related to another enduring part of human nature: imagination.

As we grow beyond childhood into adulthood, we inevitably lose that power of imagination that once made it possible to pretend we were a bird or a plane. Such total suspension of disbelief seems to slip further away from us over the years. But we don't lose it completely; a little remains, and it just needs a little help.

That's what the flight simulator provides: a tiny bit of deception, just sufficient to make us forget our everyday worries for a while and concentrate on landing at La Guardia or barnstorming the Golden Gate Bridge.

For thousands of us who are now practical, hard-working adults—perhaps with children of our own—that's enough. We're flying.

David Florance
Tom R. Halfhill
Philip I. Nelson

March, 1987

Introduction

The 48 adventures in this book are arranged roughly in order of difficulty. The first several flights let you practice basic flying skills—takeoffs, landings, climbing, descending, and simple navigation. They also introduce you to the scenery in different regions of the country which are mapped out in the flight simulator. Later adventures hone your basic flying skills and help you develop new ones—instrument-only flights and landings, more complex navigation, and even aerobatics. Some adventures lead you on sightseeing tours through the world of the simulator, pointing out features you may have missed, while others are whimsical trips included just for fun.

Before you get started, however, there are some important matters to take care of. One of the first things every pilot learns is *never*—under any circumstances—to begin a flight without first performing a number of preflight checks. These checks are intended to verify that the plane is, indeed, in perfect flying condition. Following a specific checklist, the pilot tests and examines the plane's instruments, radios, engine(s), fuel and oil levels, batteries, landing gear, control surfaces, and many other items. Only when everything on the list passes inspection does the pilot make ready for takeoff.

Fortunately, you don't have to duplicate that laborious procedure each time you sit down at the flight simulator. But there are several steps you must perform before embarking on the flight adventures in this book.

Preceding each adventure is a section that looks something like this:

Environment: Winter
Time: 10:46:00
Carb Heat: Off
Flaps: Up
Mags: Both
Lights: Off
Aircraft Orientation: On
Auto Coord: On
Sound: On
Winds:

Level 3 Tops	= 20000
Dir	= 165
Bot	= 15000
Speed	= 5
Turb	= 0
Level 2 Tops	= 10000
Dir	= 172
Bot	= 7000
Speed	= 2
Turb	= 0
Level 1 Tops	= 6000

Dir	= 166
Bot	= 4356
Speed	= 3
Turb	= 0

Surface Winds AGL:

Dpth	= 2000
Dir	= 171
Speed	= 1
Turb	= 0

Position Set:

Aircraft North	= 21371.378
East	= 6481.4524
Alt	= 377.8736
Heading	= 002

Clouds:

Level 1 Tops	= 9000
Base	= 8000
Level 2 Tops	= 10000
Base	= 9000
Ground Fog	= None

Correctly entering this information into the flight simulator is crucial to executing the adventure. If you're a veteran simulator pilot, you may already know how to do this. But if you're new to the Macintosh, Amiga, or Atari ST versions of the program, you may be unsure of how to proceed.

The manual which accompanies the flight simulator explains in full detail how to adjust these settings, but what follows is a quick summary, as well as some special notes.

Settings

You can set the season under the ENVIRO menu. Although the time of year may seem unimportant, it can actually make a big difference in the way scenery is displayed. For instance, such events as sunrise and sunset are determined by the season and time of day.

The time, of course, is set by adjusting the digital clock near the radio stack. The clock uses 24-hour military time.

Carb Heat is one of the little-used settings along the bottom of the instrument panel. It's needed in cold winter weather to keep the engine's carburetor from icing up and failing at a critical moment. Normally, Carb Heat is OFF.

Flaps are large control surfaces on the trailing edges of the wings. Unlike ailerons, though, they aren't used for steering the plane—they're employed whenever you need increased lift and drag for shorter takeoffs and landings. Normally, the flaps are left UP.

Mags are the magneto (engine ignition) switches. Normally, these switches should be set to BOTH.

Lights are the plane's exterior running lights and interior instrument panel bulbs. When night falls, most of the instrument panel becomes invisible until you switch the lights ON. During daylight hours, the lights should be left OFF to extend the life of the instrument panel bulbs. (The bulbs can burn out between servicing stops.)

Aircraft Orientation determines how the map display will be shown on the screen in relation to the plane's current direction of travel. If Aircraft Orientation is selected under the NAV menu, the map is rotated so the top is always in the direction you're flying. The alternative is *North Orientation*, where the map display always puts north at the top of the window. Normally, Aircraft Orientation is ON, but this is a matter of personal preference.

Auto Coord (automatic coordination) is found under the SIM menu. When selected, this option links the ailerons and the rudder, making the plane somewhat easier to fly. Normally it's left ON, but it must be turned OFF to perform some aerobatic maneuvers.

Sound, too, is a matter of personal preference. If you like to hear the steady drone of the engine while you're cruising, and hear audible feedback when you increase or decrease the throttle, leave the sound ON. Otherwise, refer to the digital tachometer for visual feedback of the engine speed.

Winds are set under the ENVIRO menu. Winds are important in some of the adventures to determine how the airplane will respond when flying in various directions. In other adventures, winds are turned off by setting all of the *Speed* parameters to zero. To simulate adverse weather conditions, the *Turbulence* factors are sometimes set to nonzero values.

Position Set is found under the NAV menu. The *North* and *East* coordinates determine the plane's starting location in the simulator world, and the *Alt* setting determines the plane's starting altitude. Most of the adventures begin on the ground at an airport, but a few start in midair. When an adventure begins on the ground, you can simply enter a zero for the altitude, and the simulator automatically adjusts the value for the actual ground altitude at those coordinates.

Compass Heading is the trickiest setting and one of the most important. It determines the plane's direction of flight—in other words, which way you're facing. Unfortunately, current versions of the Macintosh, Atari ST, and Amiga flight simulators have no provision for setting the compass heading. Since earlier versions of the simulator program for eight-bit computers made it quite easy to adjust the heading, the absence of this feature is evidently an oversight. To overcome this handicap, you'll have to set the heading by actually maneuvering the airplane.

If the adventure starts on the ground, open the throttle just a notch and taxi the plane right or left until the compass at the top of the instrument panel indicates the proper heading. Then close the throttle and apply the brakes.

If the adventure starts in midair, turn right or left as required and stabilize the plane on the correct heading. Then hit the pause key.

Either way, you'll have to reenter the *Position Set* coordinates and altitude settings so you can restart the adventure from the proper location. Hopefully, future versions of the flight simulator will make it possible to set the compass heading merely by entering the desired number.

Clouds and *Ground Fog* affect visibility at various altitudes and play an important role in some adventures. Usually, though, the skies are kept clear to reveal more interesting scenery.

Besides all of these settings, some adventures add special conditions, such as the Learjet aircraft instead of the Cessna. So make your preflight checks carefully.

Special note to all computer pilots using the Macintosh:

The Macintosh version of *Flight Simulator* apparently has a software flaw. One of the instruments, the ADF (Automatic Direction Finder), often shows incorrect—or at best, misleading—readings. There are only two adventures which use the ADF extensively.

"Not's Landing," in which you're told to follow course with the ADF, and "Howdy, Pilgrim," where the same applies, are the two adventures.

In both cases you should use the *radial* referred to in the text as the primary guide to course movement. In the other five or so instances where the adventures use ADF, it's there only as an additional tracking aid, and can be essentially ignored.

Please note that in all cases, care has been taken not to use ADF alone, so that the book can be applied by the owners of all three of the 68000 machines—the Macintosh, the Amiga, and the Atari ST.

In addition, the Microsoft version includes less-than-complete maps, in that all the airports available in the program are not found on the accompanying charts. Thanks to SubLOGIC for allowing us to reprint the maps from the Amiga and Atari ST versions of the program. With these charts, Macintosh owners have a full-charted view throughout the book of where they are flying.

The Adventures

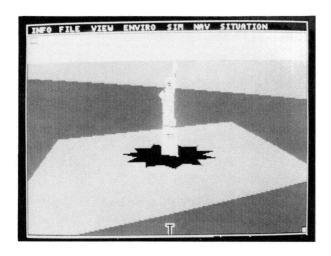

1
Lady Liberty

Environment: Summer
Time: 18:41:00
Carb Heat: On
Flaps: Up
Mags: Both
Lights: Off
Aircraft Orientation: On
Auto Coord: On
Sound: On

Winds:
Level 3 Tops	=	9500
Dir	=	310
Bot	=	7000
Speed	=	5
Turb	=	0
Level 2 Tops	=	7000
Dir	=	310
Bot	=	4000

Speed	=	5
Turb	=	0
Level 1 Tops	=	4000
Dir	=	304
Bot	=	100
Speed	=	4
Turb	=	0

Surface winds AGL:
Depth	=	100
Dir	=	310
Speed	=	2
Turb	=	0

Position Set:
Aircraft North	=	17287.000
East	=	21249.000
Alt	=	10.000
Heading	=	180

Special Instructions: None

You're at Igor I. Sikorski Airport, off the runway area. This is strictly a piloting mission. You won't be using any VOR stations, NDBs, or any other kind of navigational aid. Your destination—the Statue of Liberty, in New York Harbor.

Go ahead and make the preflight check. Here's a list of things to check before you take off on any flight.

Airspeed indicator	Radio frequencies
Altimeter	Fuel tank(s)
Throttle indicator	Oil pressure and temperature
Carb heat	Mixture control
Magnetos	Suction gauge
Ailerons	Lights
Elevators	Transponder
Rudders	Heading
Compasses	Course selector
Brakes	Clock

If everything looks OK, take off for your flight to the Lady. You shouldn't find it difficult to taxi onto the runway and line up for takeoff. (Yes, it is easier to do this if you pull down the map display, but try to do it with nothing but the window views, just like a pilot in a real plane.))

As soon as you get straightened out on the runway (the one with the big white stripes), give it full throttle for liftoff.

Immediately after takeoff, you'll see an airport disappearing from the right-rear view. That's Sikorski. Water lies ahead and to the right. Begin a right turn, toward the body of water to the right. Continue the turn until you can see the coastline you just took off from, including Sikorski and I-95, a large highway running along the water. You want to fly down the middle of this expanse of water, which is Long Island Sound.

Don't look at the map. For the time being, you'll just have to trust me as your copilot. Keep your altitude low, about 1000 feet. We don't want to miss a good view of the Lady when we reach her neighborhood.

Check your right view as you fly down the Sound. The highway is still there—use it to orient yourself. If you're flying nearly parallel to the highway, you're doing just fine. The left window should reveal what looks like one or two strips of land, with water in the far distance. Since you're not looking at the map, it's only fair to inform you that the land is Long Island.

If you made the turn and leveled out without too much delay, Sikorski should still be visible in the rear view, but shrinking steadily. I-95 appears to trail away in that direction, as well.

Back to the front view, which should show plenty of water, narrowing in the distance. Before too long, you'll catch sight of the highway as it appears to swing across the middle of the front view. Either it connects with another highway, or it turns down the coastline itself. Too soon to tell with any certainty.

Now for a few minutes of easy going along the Sound. Try to keep the plane centered above the water, about equidistant from land on both sides. Oh—by the way, did I tell you that I've never tried to find the Statue of Liberty by sight from this direction? I have a seat-of-the-pants idea of how to get there, but we'll both have to rely pretty much on our eyes for this one.

After the Sound begins to narrow, a distant airport appears to the right. Slide over to the left as needed to keep your craft over the middle of the body of water. Looks like the coastline curves gradually down to the right.

It's clear now that the Sound is bisected by a pair of bridges, with an airport on the left body of land beyond the bridges. The airport is La Guardia, but we're not going to land there. Just concentrate on keeping the plane centered over the water.

Things are getting complicated. As you come up on the first bridge, you start to see a lot more city scenery beyond La Guardia. For the time being, though, your concentration is focused mainly on keeping the craft level and centered over the ever-narrowing body of water below. Don't get careless about your altitude. If you're not holding level at 1000 feet, take care of the situation now.

La Guardia is just behind your left shoulder. Bear to the left as the water narrows even further, and you'll soon have Manhattan in view to the right. There's the Empire State Building, and here come the World Trade Center towers.

Don't lose the Sound as it empties into the Upper Bay. The last bridge you see is the Brooklyn Bridge. Now look to the right—it's Lady Liberty, all right. If she looks a bit thin to you, keep in mind that she just had a major facelift. She'll get more impressive as we draw closer.

Lose just a little altitude by pushing forward on the stick. Don't get carried away, though. Remember, you're not very far off the ground in the first place. Line up with the statue and try to level out at an altitude of about 300 feet above the water. Before long, the Lady comes into full view—a majestic sight.

See, you can trust me. Even when I don't know where I am.

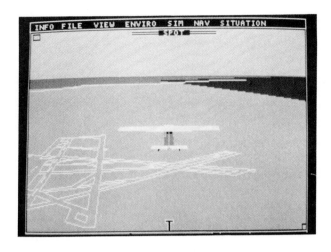

2
Boston Tea Party

Environment: Spring
Time: 15:32:00
Carb Heat: On
Flaps: Up
Mags: Both
Lights: Off
Aircraft Orientation: On
Auto Coord: On
Sound: On

Winds:
Level 3	= No winds
Level 2	= No winds
Level 1 Tops	= 6000
Dir	= 120

Bot = 100
Speed = 9
Turb = 0
Surface winds AGL:
Depth	= 100
Dir	= 190
Speed	= 3
Turb	= 0

Position Set:
Aircraft North	= 17617.000
East	= 21607.000
Alt	= 246.000
Heading	= 120

Special Instructions None

There's a knock on the door. "Sign here," says the deliverer with a smile. You open the telegram, wondering what it's all about. Here's what the telegram says:

Get your wings on STOP
Need shipment of tea by 17:00 STOP
Reschedule for departure by 15:45 for Logan STOP
Pick up cargo at Danielson STOP
See you at Logan STOP

Tea shipment? Logan by 17:00? This can't be true, you say to yourself. Then the phone rings—it's the Danielson dispatcher, saying that your shipment of tea is ready to go. Could history be about to repeat itself?

You'll have to review your flight plan. The original schedule called for you to fly a cargo of grain to Logan tomorrow morning. Not as historically resonant as tea for Boston, perhaps, but at least you knew what to expect. On the other hand, the original flight plan should work, no matter what the cargo.

Your charts for the Boston area show both Danielson and Logan. Looks like about 60 to 70 miles. We'll be sure later. According to the plan, you'll fly the Providence radial, call Logan, and then turn 90° to line up with the Boston VORTAC at 112.7. "Simple enough," you think, as you leave for the airport.

Out the windshield you see runway 11 at Danielson. The preflight check indicates that fuel's okay, ailerons are okay, carb heat is on, and you're ready for takeoff. Give it full throttle until you reach about 60 knots; then pull back gently on the stick. Liftoff.

Once in the air, you have little time for sightseeing. Check your charts and tune NAV-1 to Providence at 115.6. It shouldn't take much maneuvering to get the OBI lined up at 118.

Don't bother grabbing too much altitude. About 2000 feet is fine for this short flight. Keep a close eye on the DME. When it indicates that you're about 17 miles out of Providence, it's time to call Logan at 119.1. Logan tells you runway 22, which means you need to start a gradual 90-degree turn right about now to get lined up for the approach. Shoot for a heading of about 30° for now. Remember, you're not very far off the ground—keep a relatively constant altitude during the turn by pulling back ever so gently on the stick.

Next, tune NAV-1 to Boston VORTAC at 112.7. The DME shows that you're approximately 50 miles out of Boston. Logan says runway 22 is in use this afternoon, so you're good for a downwind approach. You're flying the reciprocal right now—or at least something close to that. Turn to a heading of about 45°.

When you're about 35 miles out, Beantown appears in the distance as a steadily expanding blob. While you watch it grow, check your altitude and level out at about 2000. As you approach Boston, I-90—the Massachusetts Turnpike—becomes visible on your left. It runs around Newton, around the north end of Brookline, right into I-93 in the city. As you approach the 20-mile mark, I-95 can be seen winding around the suburbs. Just on the other side of the junction of 93 and the Turnpike is Logan, your destination. The darker area to the right is water.

Logan Airport starts to become visible at a distance of about 11 to 15 miles. Better check with the tower again to verify your approach. Runway 22 is still okay, so the plan holds— you'll fly past Logan on the left and make two 90-degree turns to bring you back on the approach for runway 22.

As you pass Logan, nice and easy, the airport seems to float by under your left wing. Now look out over your right shoulder. When Logan appears in the far corner of your view, it's time to make the first turn.

Bring the heading around to 130° and level out; then look out your right side window at the runway. When you're almost parallel to the runway, it's time to make the final turn, right into runway 22.

As you level out of the last turn, begin the smooth glide down, using the throttle and stick together to lose altitude. You may need to crab a bit to remain on the runway heading. At a distance of two miles you can see that there are two runways on 22. You'll be using the one on the right. The altitude at Logan is about 20 feet above sea level.

It's time to bring the plane down. Once you're right at the end of the runway, drop the throttle to almost dead stick. Then put the aircraft down gently and taxi over to the service area on the right, near the terminal.

Wait a minute; where are the colonists in tricorner hats? Have you been daydreaming again? This is Boston, and you're packing a load of tea, but that's where the similarity ends. The lad who comes to check you out is wearing unmistakably modern coveralls, and probably doesn't know what a tricorner hat looks like.

Oh well, at least they still serve beans here.

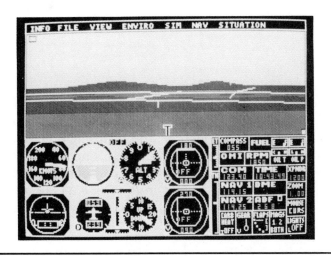

3
Washington Monument

Environment: Summer
Time: 10:30:00
Carb Heat: Off
Flaps: Up
Mags: Both
Lights: Off
Aircraft Orientation: On
Auto Coord: On
Sound: On

Winds:

Level 3 Tops	=	20000
Dir	=	165
Bot	=	15000
Speed	=	5
Turb	=	0
Level 2 Tops	=	10000
Dir	=	172
Bot	=	7000
Speed	=	2
Turb	=	0
Level 1 Tops	=	6000

Dir	=	166
Bot	=	4356
Speed	=	3
Turb	=	0

Surface winds AGL:

Depth	=	2000
Dir	=	171
Speed	=	1
Turb	=	0

Position Set:

Aircraft North	=	21371.378
East	=	6481.4524
Alt	=	377.8736
Heading	=	002

Clouds:

Level 1 Tops	=	9000
Base	=	8000
Level 2 Tops	=	10000
Base	=	9000
Ground Fog	=	None

O n to the Pacific Northwest. Here you'll get a chance to explore some of the unique features of the 16-bit flight simulator. The Northwest is an ideal place to practice bad-weather flying, radio navigation, and instrument landings. As any resident of Seattle can tell you, there's no shortage of clouds or drizzle in this area. At the same time, the lack of large cities crowded together (as in the Eastern Corridor) makes it easier to find that small, out-of-the-way airfield you may be looking for.

This initial adventure takes place on a warm summer day obscured only by some cloud cover above 8000 feet. But you should have no reason to climb that high for this flight. It's not raining, the winds aren't too strong, and it's a fine day for flying.

Start your preflight check. Your plane is resting dead-center on the runway at Port Orchard, Washington, near the battleship monument U.S.S. Missouri—the ship on which the Japanese surrender was signed in Tokyo Bay in 1945. You're about 16 miles west of Seattle.

As you take off, one of the things you'll notice about cloudy-day flying is the difference it makes in the appearance of the horizon. Sometimes, depending on your angle of attack, it will look as if you're lost in the clouds, even when you're well below the cloud cover. Don't fret—the ground will come into view as you level off.

As soon as you leave the ground and start climbing, open up the simulator's map display. Zoom it out as appropriate until you can clearly see the network of four or five highways on the right. That's Seattle. The road nearest you is I-5, which winds up the coastline all the way from San Diego to Canada. You'll also see one or two large airports to the right, near Seattle proper.

In a few minutes you'll notice two highways on the map display which run perpendicular to I-5. These are I-90 (running horizontally near the bottom) and State Route 520 (running horizontally near the top). You're going to make a right turn over the body of water there, which is Puget Sound. A couple of minutes after takeoff, before your map view indicates that you're actually over the water, come to a new heading of 030° and level off at approximately 2500 feet.

Your goal: A close-up look at the "Washington Monument," the Seattle Space Needle. The Needle is located at the 74-acre Seattle Center, site of the Century 21 World's Fair in 1962. The Space Needle is a graceful 605-foot tower capped with an observation deck. You're in for an excellent view of this landmark.

Coming out of your turn to 030°, by the way, you'll see another tall Seattle landmark: beautiful Mt. Rainier—at 14,410 feet, the highest peak in Washington.

As you fly along, Puget Sound slips beneath you. Very soon now you'll catch your first glimpse of the Space Needle. It appears as a short, nondescript vertical line at first, then gradually grows in size and becomes more obvious as you close in.

Fly straight toward the Needle, turning a bit if necessary. (Your exact angle of approach depends on how soon you made the turn to 030°.) Lose some altitude now, dropping down to about 1000 feet for a close look. As you fly by on the right side, wave to the people at the top of the Needle.

After you pass, bank into a steep left turn to circle back around the Needle. This turn should put you on a heading of 230° or so, but the exact heading will vary depending on your approach. When you come by the second time, check your various windows for different views of the Needle.

In moments you'll be flying out over Puget Sound again. As you're cruising above the water, a wicked thought suddenly pops into your mind: On that second pass, you noticed that the Needle is capped by two saucer-shaped levels—the observation deck and a restaurant. The two levels are separated by a distance of several dozen feet. The wicked thought is beginning to take shape. That gap is awfully inviting, is it not? There might be just enough room in it for a small plane...or is there? All at once you're overcome by the challenge. Should you try it? *Why not?*

Keep flying over Puget Sound until you're just about halfway across; then make a 180-degree turn. Descend to about 600 feet, level off, and keep a watchful eye on that altimeter. Line yourself up with the Needle early and adjust your course often. There won't be much time (or room) to fiddle around on this pass.

As you get closer, make any slight altitude adjustments that are necessary to aim your plane right between the two decks. They should be around 600 feet.

Now it's time to throw caution to the winds. Aim straight for that gap and say a tiny prayer. Oh, no—*look out!*

Did you make it?

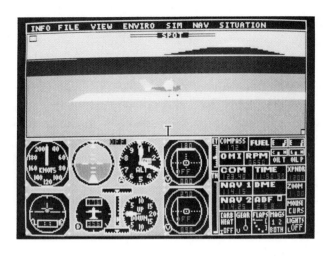

4
The Vanishing Volcano

Environment: Fall
Time: 11:36:00
Carb Heat: Off
Flaps: Up
Mags: Both
Lights: Off
Aircraft Orientation: On
Auto Coord: On
Sound: On

Winds:

Level 3 Tops	= 12307
Dir	= 136
Bot	= 6543
Speed	= 7
Turb	= 0
Level 2 Tops	= 6542
Dir	= 188
Bot	= 4532

Speed	= 6
Turb	= 0
Level 1 Tops	= 4531
Dir	= 177
Bot	= 1001
Speed	= 3
Turb	= 0

Surface winds AGL:

Depth	= 100
Dir	= 160
Speed	= 4
Turb	= 0

Position Set:

Aircraft North	= 21300.000
East	= 6480.0000
Alt	= 292.0000
Heading	= 60

Clouds: None

Check your left-front window. There it is—your target. Mt. Rainier, at 14,410 feet, the tallest peak in the state of Washington, and the fourth-highest peak in the continental United States. So majestic, so compelling. Even in the simulation it towers above the ground like a statue of dignity.

Today you'll set out on a quest for the closest possible look at the mountain—the closest possible look, that is, without crashing into it. And since the maximum rated ceiling of your single-engine Cessna 182 is only 14,900 feet, there won't be much room to spare.

Your starting point is Tacoma Narrows Airport in Tacoma, Washington. Puget Sound is directly in front of you, and Mt. Rainier lies to the southeast. Make the usual preflight checks and start rolling down the runway. As the plane reaches stall speed, about 65 knots, pull back gently on the stick. The aircraft slowly rises into the crisp fall air. Don't wait too long to lift off, because this airstrip actually extends out over the water. If you run out of runway, you'll take a bath.

As you get airborne, you immediately find yourself over The Narrows, part of the upper reaches of Puget Sound. To steer toward Mt. Rainier, turn left to a new compass heading of 100°. This puts you on a southeasterly course, and the snowcapped peak is plainly visible dead ahead.

Just in front of you are several airports: Spanaway, Shady Acres, and Pierce County. McChord Air Force Base is nearby, too. You can't see the base, but you can tune in its VOR station at frequency 109.6 on your NAV-1 radio. As the DME (Distance Measuring Equipment) shows, you're practically on top of it.

Keep ascending and flying straight toward Mt. Rainier. Meanwhile, center the TO needle on the upper OBI (Omni-Bearing Indicator). If you have trouble keeping the needle centered, you're right on course. The needle is hard to center because you're passing directly by McChord, so the radial to the VOR station changes every few seconds. Don't fly to the radial indicated on the OBI—stick to your compass heading of 100°.

When you reach 7000 feet, level off the aircraft. Although the towering volcanic cone rises over 14,000 feet above sea level, you want to approach the crest more closely before climbing higher.

Soon the top of Mt. Rainier comes more clearly into view. That snowy peak actually consists of 26 active glaciers. At the summit, volcanic steams and gases still rise from the open crater. But the mountain was formed centuries ago, and the activity that once thrust it from the earth is long exhausted. All that remains is the skeleton of a once-bubbling mire of molten rock, the frozen cauldron of a past age's Armageddon.

As you approach the commanding landmark, it becomes increasingly evident that your meager 7000-foot altitude is grossly insufficient. Raise the elevators to begin climbing over the mountain. You'll also need to open up the throttle to insure that the climb is steady.

If you look closely, and enhance the view with a dose of imagination, you may glimpse the highways that wind their way up the mountain. Mt. Rainier is a popular tourist attraction, and nearby are several resorts, including Paradise Valley.

Your altitude should be much better now—around 10,000 feet—but you still lack the necessary clearance for a safe overflight. The idea, of course, is to fly as near as possible to the ice-clad peak without becoming a permanent part of it. Give the engine full throttle and keep climbing.

Now you can see the glaciers which slowly grind their way down Mt. Rainier. They bear oddly beautiful names with varied backgrounds: Nisqually, Ingraham, Winthrop, Tahoma, Cowlitz, Paradise, Emmons. The Cowlitz and Nisqually glaciers are the most often explored, but the Paradise glacier is perhaps the most lovely. All of the glaciers feed rolling waterfalls and rapids that cut through glacial valleys. The mountain is circled by the Wonderland Trail, a 90-mile path that takes about nine days to traverse. Since 1870, climbers have made it to the top of Mt. Rainier, and there are both dangerous and not-so-dangerous routes. One can find exciting diversion in the deep caves and caverns that surround the mountain, but there are also more life-threatening adventures to be found, if such are sought.

As you soar beyond 12,000 feet, your progress noticeably slows. The aircraft seems prone to stall, and you're forced to lower the elevators a bit to compensate. You're approaching the tiny plane's operational ceiling, and its gas-powered engine is gulping for breathable air at this great height.

Undaunted, you keep flying nearer and nearer. The alluring view summons you like a siren's song.

But it's not to be. It soon becomes apparent that you'll never scale Mt. Rainier's mighty summit. The plane simply refuses to climb much beyond 13,000 feet—more than 1400 feet short of your goal.

Fanatically, you aim straight for the peak anyway. You've come this close, and you refuse to be denied.

But just as the blinding white glaciers fill the entire windshield—just as you brace yourself for the inevitable, glorious collision—something bizarre suddenly transpires. Mt. Rainier disappears!

Where did it go? Where *could* it have gone? Stupefied, you stare through the windshield. Gone!

Mystified, you check your rear view. There it is! Looming more than 14,000 feet into the heavens, Mt. Rainier is just where it's supposed to be. Somehow you flew right *through* the mountain. But how is that possible?

You'll never know. It was there, and then it wasn't. Maybe you flew to the bounds of the simulator's limited world. Or maybe the scenery artist despaired of recreating Mt. Rainier in all its magnificence and left it for you to invent the details within your imagination.

All you know for sure is that you've accomplished the impossible—you've flown right through the ancient volcano that the Northwest Indians once called *The Mountain That Was God*.

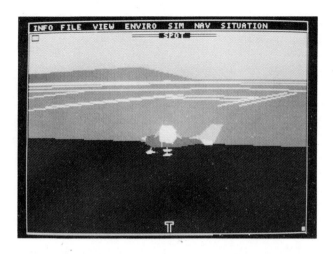

5
I Never Met a Beach I Didn't Like

Environment: Summer
Time: 12:00:00
Carb Heat: Off
Flaps: Up
Mags: Both
Lights: Off
Aircraft Orientation: On
Auto Coord: On
Sound: On

Winds:
Level 3 Tops = 32000
    Dir = 200
    Bot = 8000
    Speed = 6
    Turb = 0
Level 2 Tops = 8000
    Dir = 200
    Bot = 5000

    Speed = 9
    Turb = 0
Level 1 Tops = 5000
    Dir = 176
    Bot = 1000
    Speed = 8
    Turb = 0
Surface winds AGL:
    Depth = 1000
    Dir = 190
    Speed = 0
    Turb = 0
Position Set:
Aircraft North = 15243.947
    East = 5910.9594
    Alt = 36.0000
Heading = 193

Clouds: None

Southern California. Two hundred years ago it was the middle of nowhere, a frontier province sparsely settled by a few Hispanics and Spanish missionaries. Today it's a modern-day land of milk and honey, the center of the world's largest entertainment industry, the hip headquarters of fad and fashion. And in the summer when the surf's up, it's a land of sun and fun.

That's where you come in. For this flight adventure, you're an airborne beach bum—a Southern California tour pilot. Four times a day during the summer months you fly a small planeload of passengers from Huntington Beach to Will Rogers Beach and back again. You don't get paid much, but you love your work. The scenery is beautiful, there's no boss breathing down your neck, and your passengers think you're cool. After all, you're a glamorous pilot in mirrored sunglasses, and you know everything about the beaches that they want to know: where the action is, and where they should hang out when they visit the beaches on the ground.

On top of all that, you get to meet a lot of interesting people. On this coastline tour, you have four passengers. They're all eager to see the sights. Most of the people who take this flight are tourists from landlocked locales. Right now there's a steelworker from Pittsburgh, a college student from Butte, Montana, a schoolteacher from Phoenix, and a psychotherapist from Abilene, Kansas. Quite a crew.

You're all set to begin the tour. The plane is fueled up and idling on the runway at Meadowlark Airport in the heart of Huntington Beach, about 22 miles southeast of Los Angeles. Your takeoff on a heading of 193° will carry you over the Pacific Coast Highway and the deep blue waters of nearby Sunset Beach.

Don't fly too far out over the waters, though. Remember, this is a tour of the beaches. You should bank right and come to a new heading of about 267°. This heading is approximate and will change constantly, since your goal is to stick to the coastline as it winds its way northward. The map display will be an indispensable tool.

You must also be careful not to gain too much altitude, lest you deprive your passengers of a clear view. Try to level off at about 800 feet. Since you're flying over the ocean, you don't have to worry about any dangerous discrepancies between the sea level–based altimeter reading and the actual ground level.

As soon as you get aligned with the coastline, you'll pass by the U.S. Naval Weapons Station on your right. Although it's not clearly depicted in the simulation, it's part of the gray-colored urban sprawl that has crept right up to the waterfront.

Now's a good time to tune in your NAV-1 to the Seal Beach VOR at 115.7. You don't really need it to navigate this flight, but it's a good habit to always tune in the nearest station. And the VOR needle will indicate when you pass by Seal Beach.

Up ahead, along the shore of San Pedro Bay, is Long Beach, where the *Queen Mary* is docked. The airstrips near the horizon are at Torrance Municipal Airport in Lomita (you may have to switch to your right-front view to see them). The land jutting out across the bay is in the general area of Point Fermin, Cabrillo Beach Park, and the Long Beach Naval Shipyard.

A few twists and turns are necessary here to follow the curving coastline of San Pedro Bay. You should avoid banking *too* steeply, though, because you don't want to make your passengers airsick. Remember, the restroom facilities in a single-engine Cessna aren't too lavish.

When you pass over Point Fermin, the scenery abruptly changes to reveal Rancho Palos Verdes, Royal Palms State Beach, and Marineland. Off in the far distance, right on the horizon, are the brown peaks of the Santa Monica and San Gabriel Mountains.

The metropolis of Los Angeles with its massive network of freeways should now be clearly in sight from your front or right-front window. Keep an eye on that altimeter to maintain your ideal sightseeing altitude of 800 feet, and hone your flying skills by executing graceful, curving turns to parallel the coastline. Don't forget that your promotional literature advertises that you'll stay over the water. Your map display tucked into a corner of the screen will be a big help.

As always, there are some light winds blowing in today, but they shouldn't pose any significant problems.

After your next right turn, the beaches you encounter are Redondo State Beach, Hermosa Beach, and Manhattan State Beach, better known as the Strip. Your passengers are very interested now, as they lean toward the windows to catch a glimpse of the hundreds of sunbathers on the shore.

One of the sights they'll see from the right window is the tarmac complex of Los Angeles International Airport. You've been there many times, but you're not going there today. Out of habit, though, you tune your NAV-1 to the LAX VOR at 113.6.

As the first leg of your trip nears a close, you pass over Venice City Beach and the intricate inlets of Marina del Rey. You're a little too high to make out the skateboarders who scoot up and down the sidewalks in Venice, but (thankfully) you're also out of earshot of their boom boxes.

Finally you reach the last beach on the trip: Will Rogers State Beach, named for the famous comedian of the twenties and thirties who, as you might recall, was killed in a plane crash. To keep your passengers from remembering this piece of trivia, usually at this point you turn to them and say something like, "That's the last beach of our tour. If you ask me which beach I like best, I have to say that I never met a beach I didn't like." There's nothing that makes you think it'll be any funnier this time, but you say it anyway. The passengers politely chuckle.

For the return trip to Huntington, tune in the Seal Beach VOR at 115.7 and make a slow, sweeping U-turn. Again, the exact heading will vary as you continue to stick to the twisting coastline. You want to make sure your passengers get their money's worth.

Your plan is to fly toward the Seal Beach VOR with the dial calibrated to 220, the runway heading at Huntington. When the needle centers, you'll know that Huntington is at approximately 220. Then you can turn to 220°, and you'll just about be on runway heading for runway 22.

On the way back, you can gain some altitude if you want to give your passengers a wider view. Also, tune in the Compton NDB at 378 as a flight reference. It should be nearly straight ahead.

As the ADF needle moves, you know you're passing Compton. When you're close to Seal Beach—say, five miles away—Compton should be behind you and Meadowlark should become visible. You're intercepting this landing pattern on the base leg, so your upcoming turn will put you on final approach.

Lose some altitude at this point and hold the aircraft at about 1000 feet. As a guide, keep Meadowlark in view from the side windows. Then, while looking out of the front-right window, make your final turn at about the instant that the runway at Meadowlark disappears under your wing. This should put you on perfect heading for runway 22 and your landing.

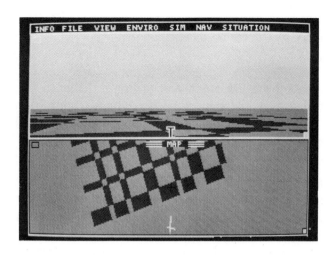

6
Monsters of the Midway

Environment: Summer
Time: 15:00:00
Carb Heat: Off
Flaps: Up
Mags: Both
Lights: Off
Aircraft Orientation: On
Auto Coord: On
Sound: On

Winds:

Level 3 Tops	= No winds
Level 2 Tops	= 9000
Dir	= 220
Bot	= 3000
Speed	= 6

Turb	= 0
Level 1 Tops	= 3000
Dir	= 220
Bot	= 1000
Speed	= 4
Turb	= 0

Surface winds AGL:

Depth	= 1000
Dir	= 220
Speed	= 5
Turb	= 0

Position Set:

Aircraft North	= 16593.499
East	= 16244.604
Alt	= 0.0000
Heading	= 114

There's nothing like the sweet aroma of Midwestern air on a balmy summer afternoon. When you're flying high above the fertile fields of the Midwest, you can sense what attracted our forefathers to the wide-open frontier. Surely these lands were the inspiration for phrases like "amber waves of grain."

On this adventure, you're taking off from Bloomington-Normal Airport in Illinois, just outside the twin cities of the same names. You'll aim for Chicago Midway, a large airport at 55th Street and Central Avenue near the heart of the Midwest's largest city. On the way, you'll see some expansive scenery that's typical of the Midwestern plains.

Watch those surface winds as you take off from Bloomington-Normal. Although there's no turbulence, the winds are stiff enough to gently rock your light plane as you climb to a cruising altitude of 3500 feet.

Almost as soon as you leave the ground, the rich farmlands of the Midwestern United States heave into view on the horizon. Soon you'll find yourself flying over vast checkerboard patterns of ripening crops. This is part of the verdant breadbasket of America—the Corn Belt. Of course, it's not just corn down there—you can find soybeans, cattle and hog farms, hay, and much more. In fact, you're flying over some of the 29 million acres of farms in Illinois.

But from 3500 feet, all you can see is the tic-tac-toe grid of fields that owe their symmetry to the meticulous planning of nineteenth-century surveyors. If you were flying over the farmlands of the Southwest, the scenery would be radically different. There, the water sprayers of modern irrigation systems turn the fields into circular islands of fertility among the arid deserts.

After enjoying the scenery for a while, tune in your NAV-1 radio to Peotone, Illinois, at 113.2. Up to now you've been heading in a southeasterly direction, which isn't exactly where you want to go to reach Chicago. After tuning in to Peotone and setting your VOR, change your heading to get back on course. Depending on where you make your turn, you may catch a view of Champaign/Urbana, home of the University of Illinois.

Pretty soon you should see Gibson City, a small town about midway between Bloomington and the Indiana border. Gibson City has two airstrips—a municipal airport and Paxton.

The practical point of this flight, in case you were wondering, is to practice getting on runway heading. Chicago Midway was chosen for this drill because it has dozens of runways in all directions. When you approach the airport, you'll call for a runway, enter the pattern (you don't know which leg you'll intercept yet), and make a landing. But this is a fairly long flight, so you can relax for now.

Since you're cruising along with nothing else to do, you might want to try some experiments with the simulator. For instance, this is an ideal time to expand the scenery window into a full-screen display. Make sure the mouse is in cursor mode. On the Amiga or Atari ST, point the mouse at the horizontal white bar separating the instrument panel from the scenery window. On the Macintosh, place the pointer on the rules at the top left of the instrument panel. Click and hold the mouse button (on the Amiga and Atari ST, the *left* mouse button); the borders of the instrument panel should start to flicker. While still pressing down the mouse button, drag the instrument panel downward until it's completely off the screen. Then release the mouse button.

The panel is gone now, but in its place is a large blank area. To fill it with scenery, point the mouse at the small square at the lower right corner of the scenery window (the square is called different names on the different machines). Again, press and hold the mouse button (*left* for Amiga/ST); then drag the flickering window toward the bottom of the screen. Release the mouse button. In a second, the scenery rescales itself and fills the entire screen.

You can enjoy this expanded view for quite a while without checking your instruments, thanks to the glacier-flattened Midwestern landscape. But we don't recommend this trick when flying over the Rockies.

To restore the instrument panel on the Amiga or Atari ST, point the mouse at the horizontal bar at the bottom of the screen. Press and hold the left mouse button; then drag the flickering window halfway up the screen. When you release the button, the instrument panel reappears and the scenery window rescales itself to its normal view.

On the Macintosh, you'll have to shrink the scenery window manually by pointing and clicking at the box in the lower right, dragging the window up, releasing the mouse button, and then clicking on the rules at the bottom of the screen (the top of the instrument panel). Keep the mouse button pressed and drag upward until the top of the panel is about halfway up the screen.

By this time you should be approaching Kankakee, Illinois, a small city on the Kankakee River. Check all of your windows for different views. If you fly directly over the city, you should be able to see Kankakee from every window.

Now it's time to tune your NAV-1 radio to Chicago Heights, 114.2. Calibrate the VOR and come to your new heading. Maintain your altitude at around 3500 feet.

You'll notice that the farm fields have disappeared as you approach the suburban sprawl enfolding metropolitan Chicago. Most likely you'll see Sanger, a small airfield, as the skyscrapers of downtown Chicago come into view. These concrete-and-glass towers form the most impressive American skyline outside of New York City. They are, perhaps, the modern-day "Monsters of the Midway," a phrase that was first applied to the Chicago Bears of 1940 after their crushing 73-0 victory over the Washington Redskins in the NFL championship.

Just beyond the skyscrapers are the dark blue waters of Lake Michigan. Another airfield you'll see in this region is Lansing Municipal, just west of the Illinois/Indiana state line.

You're close enough now to tune your COM radio to Midway ATIS at 128.05. Midway should report zulu weather with good visibility, warm temperatures, and winds 220 at five knots. The Midway tower should assign you to runway 22. (If you get another runway, you may have entered the wrong wind settings at the beginning of the simulation.)

As soon as your VOR and DME indicate that you've passed over Chicago Heights (the VOR should change itself from TO to FROM), make a quick left turn of about 90°. Your heading should now be approximately 330°. As you fly in this northerly direction, Lake Michigan should be on your right. Near the horizon, you should see a series of intersecting highways snaking across the screen. These are Interstates 57 and 80, which feed commuter traffic through Chicago's old South Side.

Don't get confused by the airfield next to I-57—that's Crestwood Howell, not Midway. Midway is located just south of I-55, which should be visible near the horizon by now. And just to the north of I-55 is I-290, the Dwight D. Eisenhower Expressway, which leads straight downtown to the Loop.

Now's the time to start losing altitude. Back off the throttle and point the nose down. In a few moments you're going to level off at about 2000 feet. What you're trying to do is intercept the Midway traffic pattern on the downwind leg.

While still descending, turn right to a heading of 040°. This is the reciprocal of the runway heading. Lake Michigan should now be directly in front of your plane, and you should have lost enough altitude during the turn to level off at 2000 feet. Downtown Chicago appears as a forest of skyscrapers on the lakefront, and the 110-story Sears Tower should be clearly visible up ahead. Another landmark is Merrill C. Meigs Airport on its artificial peninsula jutting out into the lake.

As you approach the lakefront, switch to your back view. Midway should be growing smaller and smaller in the distance. When you pass over Meigs and head out over the lake, quickly turn left 180°. You're making a giant (but legal) U-turn over downtown Chicago as the John Hancock Building and Sears Tower seem to swing by. As you come to your new heading of about 220°, Midway should be dead ahead, and you ought to be straight in line with runway 22.

When you get close to Midway, you'll notice that it's crisscrossed with dozens of runways in all directions. Runway 22 actually consists of 22 left, 22 right, and several others. Pick the one you're most nearly lined up with, and make your approach. The runway with the stripes is probably the widest. They're all fairly long, so you should have plenty of room to make a good landing.

After safely touching down, turn right to taxi toward the terminal. If you see a blinking light on the runway, turn right at that point and you can't miss it. The terminal is a low gray building, and the buildings of downtown Chicago should be visible in the distance.

At this point, we highly recommend catching a cab to Water Tower Place, where you can buy a sandwich and enjoy the street comedians, singers, and dancers who inevitably perform for donations around the historic Water Tower on summer evenings. This is where the great Chicago fire of 1871 was turned back, and the urban atmosphere along Michigan Avenue's "Magnificent Mile" is a startling contrast to the Midwestern farmlands you toured this afternoon.

7
Not's Landing

Environment: Summer
Time: 16:45:00
Carb Heat: Off
Flaps: Up
Mags: Both
Lights: Off
Aircraft Orientation: On
Auto Coord: On
Sound: On

Winds:
Level 3 Tops = No winds
Level 2 Tops = 5000
    Dir = 330
    Bot = 2000
   Speed = 5

    Turb = 0
Level 1 Tops = 2000
    Dir = 330
    Bot = 1000
   Speed = 4
    Turb = 0
Surface winds AGL:
   Depth = 1000
    Dir = 330
   Speed = 2
    Turb = 0
Position Set:
Aircraft North = 15495.000
    East = 5810.0000
    Alt = 804.00000
Heading = 351

S tarting at Van Nuys Airport in Los Angeles, you're bound for
Compton Airport—just 20 miles on the other side of town.
Why fly only 20 miles? Notice the time—16:45:00, or a quar-
ter till five. And it's a Friday afternoon, to boot. Have you
ever tried driving from Van Nuys to Compton on the San
Diego Freeway (I-405) at rush hour? That's why you're flying.

At least, that's one of the reasons. The other reason will
be a surprise.

When the adventure starts, you're sitting on an access
road at Van Nuys Airport. You'll have to taxi onto runway 34.
But first, switch on your ADF and adjust it to 378. The ADF is
crucial for this flight.

Open up your map display and zoom in until you can see
the runways at Van Nuys. Turn right and taxi forward a few
feet; then turn left to line up with the runway into the wind.
Your compass heading should now be about 343°. Take off
and start climbing to an altitude of about 1000 feet (about 200
feet above ground level).

Very soon you'll hear a series of beeps if you're using the
Amiga or Atari ST; on the Macintosh, the Outer marker indicator lights up. Both the tones and the light mean that you've
overflown the Outer marker on the ILS at Van Nuys. While
continuing to climb, make a smooth, gradual turn toward the
right until the ADF needle rests solidly on the zero. This
brings you around almost 180° from the direction of your
takeoff. During the turn, you'll glimpse a lot of scenery: the
Van Nuys Airport, various freeways, and some mountain
ranges. Don't turn too fast; there's no hurry, and you don't
want to risk losing altitude at this height.

After you complete your turn, keep climbing until you
reach about 3500–4000 feet.

All you have to do to stay on course during this flight is
keep that ADF needle on zero. This requires minor course corrections from time to time because of the winds and your angle of approach. Just remember to keep an eye on the needle.

Among the sights you'll see next are the San Gabriel Mountains. If you're on course, you should be a safe distance away from their dangerous peaks.

After a while, you'll pass by Los Angeles International Airport (LAX), which might be visible on the horizon out of your right window. You'll also pass near Hawthorne Municipal Airport, which is much smaller than LAX, but probably more visible because it's closer.

Pretty soon now, Compton should come into view straight ahead. If you stay exactly on course, it may be visible just slightly on the left side of your front window. Beyond the airport you'll see the deep blue waters of the Pacific Ocean.

Wait until Compton almost disappears below your front view. You're going to enter the pattern downwind. Just before Compton disappears, start turning left—not too quickly, not too slowly. You'll see a mountain roll by, and then another range of mountains will appear. Come out of the turn to a new compass heading of 055°.

Switch to the rear view. You should see Compton behind you, and its two landing strips should be apparent. (If the strips look a little fuzzy, you may be too high—remember to stay around 3500–4000 feet.)

Hopefully, you're still on course. Ideally, the rear view should show Compton between the tail of the plane and the left edge of the window. When it's exactly halfway between the two, turn right to a heading of 140°.

Now glance out of your right window. The Compton airstrips should be clearly visible and just ahead of your position. Don't waste precious moments admiring the view, though, because it's time for yet another turn.

Switch back to the front window and start turning right to a heading of about 230°. The heading is approximate because your goal is to line up perfectly with the runways, so make any adjustments that you deem necessary.

At this point, if skill (and luck) have been your copilots, you *should be* making a perfect approach.

But remember a while ago, when we promised a surprise? You might recall that this adventure is entitled "Not's Landing." One reason is that the TV show "Knot's Landing" is placed near Compton. The other reason is that you're *not* going to land at Compton after all.

Instead, you're going to attempt a tricky maneuver known as a *touch'n'go*. Do everything as if you were going to land here, but at the very last moment—when you hear your tires screeching on the pavement—instantly throttle up to take off again.

If you can master this technique, you're just one step away from being able to make a landing. In fact, this is a good way to learn how to make perfect landings.

So throttle down, drop your nose, and make your final approach.

Did you make it? If you successfully pulled off your first touch'n'go, congratulations! You're almost ready for the big leagues.

On the other hand, if you wound up nose-first in the ground at Compton—and most pilots will on the first try— you need more practice. That's a "Not's Landing" of the wrong kind.

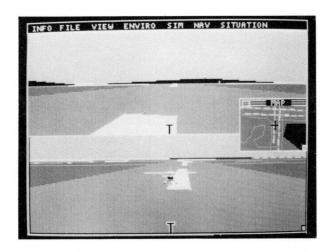

8
The Grand Tour

Environment: Spring
Time: 12:32:00
Carb Heat: On
Flaps: Up
Mags: Both
Lights: Off
Aircraft Orientation: On
Auto Coord: On
Sound: On

Winds:

Level 3 Tops	= 5998
Dir	= 399
Bot	= 3999
Speed	= 5
Turb	= 0

Level 2 Tops	= 3999
Dir	= 297
Bot	= 3796
Speed	= 7
Turb	= 0
Level 1 Tops	= 3796
Dir	= 321
Bot	= 1000
Speed	= 4
Turb	= 0

Surface winds AGL: No winds
Position Set:

Aircraft North	= 17339.003
East	= 5058.2808
Alt	= 10.3744
Heading	= 19

Now it's time to explore some new features of Flight Simulator II—features that weren't available in the less-sophisticated versions for eight-bit computers like the Commodore 64, Atari, IBM PC, and Apple II. We'll begin by taking the next several adventures combined into one large adventure called *The Grand Tour*.

Leg 1: Oakland International

The first leg of the tour starts at San Francisco International, a huge airport just east of San Bruno and south of San Francisco. You're on the runway, ready to take off. For runway clearance, call the tower at 126.0. Then tune in Oakland VOR at 116.80, and set the OBI needle to center at 30. With a heading of about 19°, give the plane some throttle and lift off.

You're going to take a look at Oakland International, just across the bay. Level off at 1500 feet. You'll perform another touch'n'go maneuver at Oakland Airport.

Look out your right-front window to see Oakland. It doesn't look like much at this range—just some light-colored lines on the peninsula. Turn right to a heading of about 70° and descend to 1200 feet. When the DME shows about four miles, the disk will whir, and the airport will come into view. The long strip along the bay is Oakland, but you'll be landing at the north field—just beyond and to the rear of Oakland. Look out the left window as you pass the airport.

As you look under the left wing, you'll begin to lose sight of the airport. Turn left to 330°; then line up with the runway.

Remember, touch'n'go involves touching ground as if you were landing, though you only let your wheels meet the ground before taking off again. Lose altitude and approach the runway just as if you were going to land. As soon as you hit the ground, throttle up again.

Make sure your wings are straight as you leave Oakland. Look out the back window for a nice view of the airport. Just in front of you is San Leandro Bay. Don't stop off for a swim—there's still a lot of ground to cover.

You've finished the first leg of the tour. Pause the simulation or save the situation to disk before you continue.

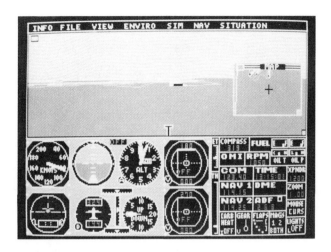

9
The Grand Tour
Leg 2: Buchanan

You've just left Oakland with a touch'n'go. Now it's on to the second airport in The Grand Tour—Buchanan Field in Concord, California.

Tune in the Concord VOR at 117.0. It should come in at about 20 miles. The signal may be a bit hard to read, but try to find the radial. As you approach downtown Oakland, you can see the Oakland Bay Bridge stretching across the bay.

As you come even closer, the disk drive whirs, and two large buildings come into view. Let's investigate. Descend to 700 feet and fly on the radial to Buchanan. The radial should be somewhere around 20°–30°. Now, adjust your heading to fly right betwen the two buildings. Below you is downtown Oakland; to the west is San Francisco Bay. Look out your windows and enjoy the view.

Now back to the front view and on to Buchanan airfield. Let's hope you didn't lose too much altitude while you were busy scanning the Bay. Center the OBI needle for Buchanan and turn to that heading; it should be somewhere in the 25°–35° range.

As you make this turn, you'll see what looks like a mountain range in the front and right views. Rather imposing, isn't it? You'd better fly over it, since there's no way to tell exactly how high the range is.

Throttle up and elevate, and look down as you pass over the high ground. These are the Berkeley Hills—not a mountain range, after all, but you still wouldn't want to run into them. The rear view shows Oakland and San Francisco. Go back to the front view and maintain the heading for Concord. At a distance of about 13 miles, the simulator goes to disk, and new scenery appears.

Level out at 4400 feet. You'll see a highway in the distance. Buchanan lies on the other side of the highway. When the field becomes visible, call the tower at 124.7 for runway information. You're assigned to runway 32. Descend to 2000 feet. You'll fly around the airport and enter the crosswind pattern.

Keep an eye on the airport first through the right-front view, then to the right. As Buchanan appears under the right wing, turn to a heading of 50°. Look out the right rear window. As the airport appears in the middle of the screen, turn right another 90°, to a heading of 140°. You're on the downwind approach.

Keep checking the view out the right window. When the airport is centered in the view, make another 90-degree turn right, to a heading of 240°, for the base leg of your approach. Then switch to the right-front view and watch until the airport is centered in your view.

At this point, it's time to turn 90° right, to a heading of 320°, for the final approach. Line up with the large runway on the right or with the smaller one on the left, whichever is more convenient.

This is a touch'n'go, too, just like the one at Oakland. Drop your throttle, lose altitude, and raise your elevators; then throttle up again when you hear the tires screech.

How did you do? You'll get better at this touch'n'go business as The Grand Tour progresses. The second leg of the tour is now complete.

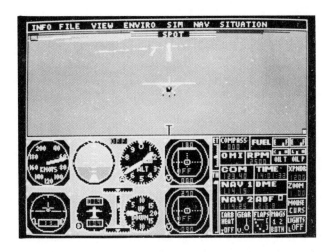

10
The Grand Tour
Leg 3: Napa County

You're flying the third leg of The Grand Tour. To the rear, Buchanan Field at Concord, California, is disappearing from view. Tune in Point Reyes VOR at 113.7. Turn to the radial indicated as you center the needle of the OBI. It will probably be in the vicinity of 250–260; the DME should read a little more than 40 miles. Level out at 3000 feet. Your destination is Napa County, California, where there's a fairly large airport that's good for practice.

San Pablo Bay is the large body of water below your path. The visible highways are parts of I-80 and its loop system. This network of roadways connects the San Pablo Bay area with its surrounding cities, towns, and counties.

At about 37 miles from the Point Reyes VOR, the Napa County Airport comes into view. As soon as it becomes visible, turn right to a heading of 270° and descend to 1500 feet.

Look out the right window. As the view of the airport starts to slip under your wing, turn right to 0° and do a touch'n'go at Napa County.

Was that easier than you had expected? If it was, the reason may be that Napa County is a large airport. It's ideal for practice—so much so, in fact, that you're going to turn around and do another touch'n'go at the same strip.

Back in the air again. Look out your back window. Perhaps you can't see the airport any more—it doesn't matter. Level out at 2500 feet. Look front again and make a left turn back to a heading of 270°. Now look right, and fly a few miles until the sight of the Napa airport slips past your right wing.

Make another 90-degree turn to a heading of 180°. You're now on the downwind for Napa County. Keep watching through your left-front window. As the field vanishes from that view, look directly out the left window. The airport looks like a huge arrow on the ground. As you continue to watch, San Pablo Bay appears larger, too. In the far distance are San Francisco and Oakland.

Back to the matter at hand. Napa is probably far enough below that you'll have to look out the left-rear window to see it. As the end of the airport reaches approximately the middle of your view, make a 90-degree turn to 90° to form your base leg. Now observe your position straight out the left window. As you look toward the wing—just before you lose sight of Napa—turn to the final approach at runway heading 0°.

Make your descent gradually, lining up constantly with the runway as you move in. Bring the craft in smoothly. A little less throttle, a little more elevator. When you hear the wheels screech, throttle up and prepare for the next leg of The Grand Tour.

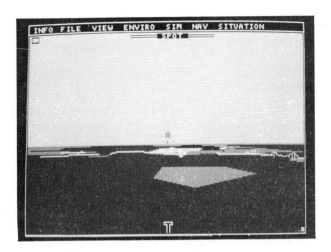

11
The Grand Tour
Leg 4: Nimitz Field

On with The Grand Tour, which so far has taken us along a skipping, crescent-shaped path: across San Francisco Bay to Oakland International, from there to Buchanan Field in Concord, then across San Pablo Bay to Napa County Airport. Our next destination is Nimitz Field.

If you performed all the touch'n'go maneuvers suggested at the end of the last adventure, your heading should be close to 000°, which should take you in the direction of Nimitz. If you got carried away at Napa, or did some extracurricular sightseeing, adjust your heading as needed.

Find Nimitz Field by tuning in to San Francisco VOR at 115.8, and flying the expanse of water that empties into San Pablo Bay. Enlarge the map display to help you follow the Bay. San Francisco won't come in immediately—it's out of range. But all the Bay Area is in the general direction of 190°. Fly that radial until San Francisco comes into range. You may have to adjust your heading slightly to keep flying over water. Level out at 2500 feet, a good cruising altitude. Within about 23 miles of San Francisco, you'll see several buildings on the horizon. Soon you'll need to make a slight turn to approximately 180°. At this distance, Nimitz appears as a few horizontal lines at the left side of the screen and to the right of the buildings.

Turn left to 150°–160° and head straight for Nimitz. There's another touch'n'go coming up. To get within range, fly so that the airport is at the left edge of your front view. You'll fly right over the Bay Bridge as you approach Nimitz.

As you approach the field, take a good look through the left windows at the airport. As you can see from the charts, Nimitz has a distinctive runway configuration. Your heading should be about 130° to 140° at this point. Watch as the view of the airport slips under the left wing. When it does, turn left to a heading of 100°. This maneuver puts you on a downwind pattern for the airport.

Look out the back windows—Nimitz is fading out of view. Turn around to a heading of about 280° and line up with the runway. The winds may hold you up a bit, but hang in there. As you approach Nimitz, a wonderful view of the Bay Area unfolds to the rear. Don't enjoy it for too long, or you might experience an unhappy landing. Remember, this is a touch'n'go, like the other touchdowns in The Grand Tour.

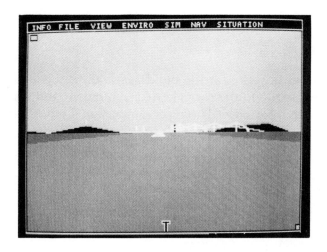

12
The Grand Tour
Leg 5: Half Moon Bay

Your next stop on The Grand Tour is Half Moon Bay, a small airport to the southeast of San Francisco, on the other side of the peninsula. Later in this book, you'll experience an adventure of great excitement involving this airstrip. So let's take a look.

You're over Nimitz Field, heading toward the Bay Area. The city up ahead is San Francisco, and the view in front of you is one of the most striking in the entire simulator world. Go ahead and fly toward the city.

Several buildings appear below. Fly down for a close look as you pass. The bridge to the right is the San Francisco–Oakland Bay Bridge. Descend to 500 feet and fly as close to the buildings as you like. Don't hit any of them, however—that's as good as hitting the ground or any other solid object.

As soon as you clear the buildings in downtown San Francisco, switch to the rear view for a moment and watch them recede from view. The three-dimensional effect is truly striking.

Now it's on to Half Moon Bay. Fly out over the water until the sight of the coastline disappears beneath your plane; then throttle up and raise the elevators, leveling out at about 2500 feet. Right now you want to fly seaward, past the Golden Gate Bridge and the peninsula. The map view makes it easy to keep your bearings.

To get a bead on Half Moon Bay, tune in Woodside VOR at 113.9. Center the needle on the OBI and turn to the heading indicated, but make sure you're over the water (the ocean, not the bay) before you make the turn. Use the map view if you're uncertain about your exact position. The plan is to fly parallel along the coast, down to Half Moon Bay.

Woodside is some 20-odd miles distant at this point, but we're not going all the way there. Your heading is in the 160°–170° range once you get lined up with the coast. If you want to make doubly sure of your heading, tune the ADF to Pigeon Point at 286—the needle should point close to the 0 mark.

Soon, an airstrip comes into view on the coastline, right where the land juts out into the sea a little. Stick to the coastline until the airstrip almost disappears from the front view. Then turn left slightly to get it back in view, and descend to 1000 feet.

If it seems that we're departing from normal landing procedures, you're absolutely right. You're not going to land at Half Moon Bay just yet. Maneuver closer to the runway and take a good look. You'll return to this port in a later adventure.

When you fly over Half Moon Bay Airport, your heading should be somewhere around 120°. If it isn't, adjust your course as needed to prepare for the next leg of the tour.

13
The Grand Tour
Leg 6: San Carlos

The previous leg of The Grand Tour began with a hair-raising joyride through downtown San Francisco and ended with a peaceful look at Half Moon Bay on the coast. Now you're headed for a landing at San Carlos, a small strip on the west side of San Francisco Bay. It's located in San Mateo County at the city of the same name, which is a suburb of San Francisco proper.

To get to San Carlos from your current position (heading 120°, just south of Half Moon Bay Airport), make a left turn to heading 30°. Increase altitude and level out at 2500 feet.

After the turn, you'll see two highways stretching across the expanse of land—I-280 and U.S. 101. San Carlos lies just east of U.S. 101, the second of the two highways from your vantage point.

Directly ahead of you, on the other side of the peninsula, is San Francisco International. Just before you pass over that airport, turn right to heading 120°. San Carlos is visible in the distance as soon as you've completed the turn. Compared to SF International, the strip seems miniscule, but it provides all the room you'll need to touch down. You're on final approach for runway 12.

The highway in front of you is Highway 92. If you look carefully, out the front or left-front view, you'll see the San Mateo Bridge, a tollway that stretches from Foster City to Hesperian Boulevard in Alameda County across the bay.

The altitude at San Carlos is just above sea level. Line yourself up with the runway and lose altitude for the final approach. This strip is narrow and quite short, so slow down the craft for a good landing. Let it drift at about 65 knots, just above stall speed. San Carlos is a classic example of a strip that calls for a precision landing, which is why you're here today. Just as you come above the end of the runway, let the airplane float down by releasing the throttle almost completely.

When you can make this landing, you're a real computer pilot. If you missed, try it again. On to the next leg.

14
The Grand Tour
Leg 7: Hayward

If you missed the landing at San Carlos, but you want to go ahead anyway, you have my permission. But you'll reap little honor in the Pilots' Hall of Fame if you skip a landing. Another option is to start over on the ground. Type in the coordinates for San Carlos from the chart and begin on the ground with a heading of 120°. Taxi to the end of the runway—this one isn't very long. Perform the usual preflight checks and then zoom down the runway. Let the engine come up to full speed before you try to leave.

Once in flight, turn around to get lined up for the next stop. It's Hayward Air Terminal, an enjoyable place to fly into—a large airfield with two gigantic runways.

Level off at 2500 feet, which should be a familiar cruising altitude by now. Tune in the Oakland VOR at 116.8. Center the OBI needle and fly to the radial indicated. You'll probably have to turn to the right to reach that heading. By pointing toward Oakland, you'll have room to turn onto the approach heading once you near Hayward. The idea is to fly past Hayward in the direction of Oakland, then turn back to the right for a landing on Hayward's runway 10.

When you first tune in Oakland VOR, the DME should read something over 12 miles. Hold a steady course until the airport comes into view. You'll be over water most of the time. At about 11 miles from Oakland, Hayward Air Terminal becomes visible in the right view. Also visible are the San Mateo Bridge, stretching across the bay, and Walpert Ridge, a large hill to the east of Hayward. Watch Hayward for a few minutes; then return to the front view.

Oakland International is easy to spot from the air, particularly from your position over San Francisco Bay. One long runway stretches out into the bay, with three shorter ones beyond. Head straight for the airport. As it begins to slip out of your front view, turn right to heading 20°.

You're now on the base leg of the approach to Hayward, which should be visible through the right window. Just before the runway appears straight in the right view, turn to heading 100° and begin to descend. If you're not confident about landing yet, use the rightmost runway, which is bigger. In the last leg of The Grand Tour, you'll be visiting San Jose.

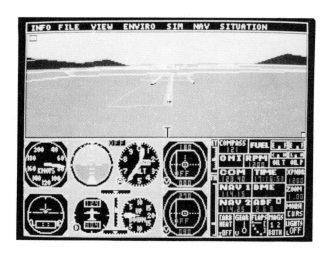

15
The Grand Tour
Leg 8: San Jose

Your final stop in The Grand Tour is San Jose International, a midsized airport south of San Francisco Bay. You finished the previous leg of the tour on the ground at Hayward Air Terminal, which lies northeast of your final destination. Taxi around so you can take off in the same direction from which you came. Tune in San Jose VOR at 114.10, make the preflight checks, and take off.

As you gain altitude, your heading is about 105°. The scenery appears sparse at first, but gains detail before too long. When it does, you'll see two highways stretching into the distance ahead—I-280 and State Highway 17. To your right is the lower end of San Francisco Bay.

Level off at 2500 feet and center the OBI needle to orient yourself for San Jose International. The needle should settle somewhere in the 130°–140° range. Fly to the heading indicated on the OBI. You can make this a leisurely turn, if you like. You're still some 15 miles from San Jose.

As you draw closer to your destination, an airport appears to the right. That's Moffett Field Naval Air Station, a fairly sizable airport that we'll visit later in this book. For now, look straight ahead and wait for San Jose to come into view.

When the DME shows about eight miles, Fremont Field appears as a short, single strip on your left. San Jose comes into view at around four miles out. Take advantage of this straight approach to get lined up well in advance. The airport has three parallel runways. You want the longest one, which lies in the middle. Remember, you're already on final approach, so don't worry about making any turns. Just line up as well as you can and start a gradual descent.

You're actually going to make two landings here. The first will be a touch'n'go, and the second will end the tour. The first touch'n'go will give you a good look at the airport. Frequently, on this tour, you've made approaches to airports using the reciprocal of the runway that would be suggested by air traffic controllers. To make navigation easier, you've ignored protocol on strips that have no simulated air traffic control tower. In other words, you've cheated—but only because I led you astray. And, like a good pilot, you followed the flight plans exactly, making all those reciprocal landings.

There's some method in this madness, however, and it begins here. After making the touch'n'go at San Jose, you're to fly over the city and get a good look at the scenery. Then you'll fly back through all the Grand Tour stops in reverse order, this time making proper landings where you failed to do so earlier. This means you can explore the region on your own, and practice for the adventures that come later in this book. You'll be a better pilot after the experience—I promise.

You should be very close to San Jose by now. Remember, this one is a touch'n'go. Line up with the central runway and lose altitude. Notice, as you come in, that there are several buildings on the horizon—they represent the city of San Jose.

Make your touch, throttle up, and go. Fly toward the buildings. Level off at 300 feet, or you'll be too high for optimum sightseeing. After your scenic tour of the city, turn around and fly back to San Jose International for a real landing. Then help yourself to as many of the tour stops as you like, in reverse order. You may even decide to stop off at some nearby fields which we didn't visit before. When you're done, take a well-deserved rest and proceed to the next adventure.

16
Teacher's Pet

Environment: Spring
Time: 18:04:00
Carb Heat: Off
Flaps: Up
Mags: Both
Lights: Off
Aircraft Orientation: On
Auto Coord: On
Sound: On

Winds:

Level 3 Tops	=	8875
Dir	=	278
Bot	=	6668
Speed	=	23
Turb	=	0
Level 2 Tops	=	6667
Dir	=	290
Bot	=	3413
Speed	=	14
Turb	=	0
Level 1 Tops	=	3412

Dir	=	349
Bot	=	1001
Speed	=	12
Turb	=	0

Surface winds AGL:

Depth	=	1000
Dir	=	260
Speed	=	10
Turb	=	0

Position Set:

Aircraft North	=	21739.000
East	=	6377.0000
Alt	=	282.0000
Heading	=	265

Clouds:

Level 1 Tops	=	20000
Base	=	10000
Level 2 Tops	=	9999
Base	=	7000
Ground Fog	=	None

I t's near dusk at William R. Fairchild International Airport at Port Angeles, Washington. Your flight instructor has just stomped off in a snit because of your poor landing skills. (You argued that in this day and age *all* runways should be at least 10,000 feet long, but he didn't buy it.) So what do you do? Frustrated, you decide to break the rules and squeeze in some practice on your own. You've got half an hour before dark—plenty of time.

You settle yourself down and make the preflight checks. Your main worry is the cloud cover; whenever you look at the sky and don't see the sun, you get a little nervous. (You've been nervous quite often lately, since moving to Washington from Miami.) But you won't let the clouds stop you. Why, with just a little more practice, you might even turn things around and become the teacher's pet.

All you have to do to qualify is make two successful landings in a row. That's all. Just two. You've made some fine landings, yes, but the following one is always flawed. Sometimes there's a nasty bump and a skid. Other times, you just seem to run out of runway. But this time you're going to do it: two in a row. Flawlessly.

Roll down the runway under full throttle, watching the airspeed indicator. When it reaches 80 knots, gently pull back on the elevators to lift off. It's funny, but takeoffs have never been a problem for you—just landings. But not even the landings this time. Two in a row or bust!

The routine is simple. Level off at 4500 feet by cutting the throttle to about 1750 rpm when you break 4000 feet. This keeps you well below the 7000-foot base of the cloud cover, so the Strait of Juan de Fuca will be clearly visible as a crescent-shaped body of water from your front view. Steer to a compass heading of approximately 270°.

Once you've leveled off, make a 90-degree left turn to heading 180°. When making a turn, remember to center the ailerons when the plane is tilted at a good turning angle (no more than 45°, as judged visually from the actual or artificial horizon). To correctly come out of the turn, you *close the bank*—that is, you start to level off about 10° before reaching the desired compass heading. In this case, you close the bank when the compass reads 190°. Make any final adjustments that may be necessary to reach the desired heading of 180°.

Now switch to your left-rear view and watch the airport, which should be visible in the distance. When it appears to be about one-third of the way across from the right edge of the window, switch back to your front view and turn left another 90°. (You should always refer to the front view when making turns, until you become *very* good.) Use the same technique as for the last turn, centering your ailerons and closing the bank about 10° before the desired heading, which is 090° on your compass.

When you level off after this turn, the airport may be visible at the left edge of your front view. If not, switch to the left-front view. It should definitely be visible there. Now watch the airport from your left windows. It will seem to creep by, passing from the left-front to the left to the left-rear windows. Don't worry—it's not going to get away; you're just waiting for the right moment to set up your final approach.

Again, when the airport appears to be about one-third of the way across from the right edge of the left-rear window, it's time to turn. Steer left yet another 90° to a compass heading of 000°. Review the names of the legs in your mind...crosswind after the first turn, downwind after the second, base leg after the third, and final approach after the fourth. Right now you're on the base leg, preparing for final.

Time to lose altitude. Cut the throttle to about 1600 rpm. It will increase as you descend, of course. Drop the elevators a notch or so to assist the descent. The VSI (vertical speed indicator) should fall below 0.

While descending, watch the airport from your left-front window, then from the left. The runway that appears to be roughly parallel with your left wing is the goal. Before you're even with this runway—again, when the airport is in the right third of your view—make a 90-degree left turn for final approach. Your final compass heading should be 270°, directly into the wind.

Continue to lose altitude. Don't drop *too* fast, though, because it's hard to regain altitude and then come back down without overshooting. Simultaneously, make whatever final adjustments are required to line up with the runway. Because of the numerous variables involved in the previous four turns, some corrections will almost certainly be called for in order to make a perfect approach.

Adjust, adjust, adjust. Gradually ease off the throttle while stepping down the elevators, and avoid any sudden movements. You'd better be lined up pretty well with the runway when you descend below 1500 feet, because the plane responds sluggishly at low altitudes.

Also, don't forget that the ground altitude at Fairchild is 282 feet above sea level. That means you have to subtract 282 from the altimeter reading to determine your actual height above the ground. If the altimeter reads 600, you're actually only about 300 feet above the earth. Forgetting this fact can lead to an unexpected merger with the pavement.

At the last possible moment, cut the throttle and tap the elevators up to raise the nose until you touch down. When you hear the tires screech on contact, hit the brakes.

You've made it—a perfect landing. And if you can do it once, you can do it twice. Repeat the flight and see if you can become the teacher's pet.

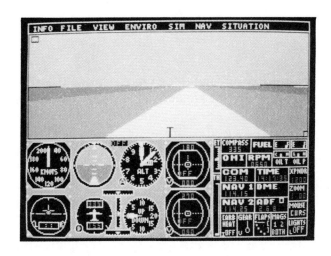

17
An Instrumental Technique

Environment: Winter
Time: 14:16:00
Carb Heat: Off
Flaps: Up
Mags: Both
Lights: Off
Aircraft Orientation: On
Auto Coord: On

Sound: On

Winds: None

Position Set:
Aircraft North = 21612.163
      East = 6735.3042
      Alt = 144.8736
Heading = 340

In this adventure you'll get some practice using ILS—the Instrument Landing System. Mastering your instruments is a critically important step in becoming an expert pilot, because eventually you'll be faced with the unpleasant task of landing in pitch darkness or in bad weather. For this practice flight, though, we've arranged for nearly perfect weather—at 43 degrees it's a little chilly, but there are no winds or clouds. Another convenience is that the flight is very short, to encourage practice through repetition.

Your starting point is the runway at Arlington Municipal, a small airport in northwestern Washington state. Your destination is Paine Field in Snohomish County, a short distance to the south. But instead of flying there on a direct path by visual flight rules, you'll make a few instrument-guided maneuvers and an instrument-only landing to sharpen your piloting skills.

Your initial runway heading is 340°. Before taking off, tune three radios: NAV-2 to the Paine VOR at 114.20, NAV-1 to the Paine localizer frequency at 109.30, and COM to the Snohomish County ATIS at 128.65. The Snohomish tower reports that the ILS runway is 16, which just happens to be the reciprocal of your current heading.

Get off the ground and quickly climb to 2500 feet. While climbing, set the OBI needle for NAV-1 to center at 160. Keep flying on your takeoff heading of 340° until the DME (Distance-Measuring Equipment) indicates that you're 21 miles from the Paine localizer frequency. (Yes, for the moment you're flying in the wrong direction.)

Now for the first tricky maneuver. When you're exactly 21 miles out from Paine, turn left to 270°. Continue flying on this radial for several minutes until the NAV-1 OBI needle starts to center. Just before it centers, quickly turn left again to heading 160°.

There's only a little room for error when you're making these two turns. If you miss the maneuver high—that is, if the NAV-1 OBI needle still lies slightly right of center after the second turn—come to 167° and fly until the needle centers more closely. Then nudge over left to 160°. On the other hand, if you miss this maneuver low—if the needle is slightly left of center after the second turn—come to 153° and fly until it centers. Then scoot over right to 160°.

If you're skillful (or lucky), the OBI needle will be exactly centered after the second turn. Whatever happens, the needle must be centered by the time the DME reads 15 miles out.

Descend to 2400 feet. Now take a look at the NAV-1 OBI dial. You'll notice a horizontal bar, although it may be hard to distinguish since it's at the very top of the dial. This is the bar to watch. It's the glideslope indicator, and it will guide your descent all the way down to the runway at Paine Field. When the DME reads about 11.5 miles out, the bar starts to move downward. At about 10.9 it moves down further. And around 9.0, the glideslope indicator should center while Paine Field's Outer marker starts beeping (or blinking). This means that it's time to cut your throttle and begin a steady descent.

The glideslope indicator is the key to smooth instrument landings. All you have to do is follow the bar. If the bar goes below the center line, you're too high, and you need to drop down to bring it back to center. If the bar goes above the center line, you're too low, and you need to pull up to center it. Check the glideslope indicator every five seconds and adjust accordingly—the bar can move very quickly if your descent is too abrupt.

Just so you don't start thinking that instrument landings are a cinch, here's another consideration: You also have to keep the OBI's *vertical* bar centered. In other words, the horizontal glideslope indicator and vertical OBI needle should form a perfect cross in the middle of the OBI dial. (At least, that's how it works for *front-course* ILS landings, which is the type you're doing now.) If the vertical needle moves left of center, turn left 25° and back again to 160° when it centers. If the needle moves right of center, turn right 25° and back again to 160° when it centers.

When the DME shows that you're just under one mile out, Paine Field's Middle marker indicator will sound off or light up. You should be able to see the airport quite clearly now. But don't pay much attention to what you're seeing outside the window—yet. Keep your eyes glued to that OBI dial, and keep those indicators centered. Remember, if this were a bad-weather flight, you probably wouldn't be able to see past your windshield anyway.

Finally, when you're right on top of the runway, cut the throttle and bring her down. A friendly chirp of rubber should be your greeting on a perfect landing. But if you crashed, try again—instrument landings are an instrumental technique to master.

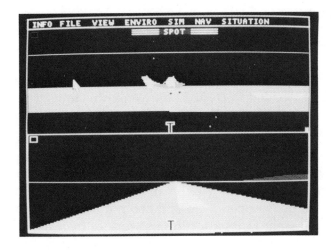

18
Space Needle

Environment: Summer
Time: 22:30:00
Carb Heat: Off
Flaps: Up
Mags: Both
Lights: On
Aircraft Orientation: On
Auto Coord: On
Sound: On

Winds:

Level 3 Tops	=	20000
Dir	=	165
Bot	=	15000
Speed	=	5
Turb	=	0
Level 2 Tops	=	10000
Dir	=	172

Bot	=	7000
Speed	=	2
Turb	=	0
Level 1 Tops	=	6000
Dir	=	166
Bot	=	4356
Speed	=	3
Turb	=	0

Surface winds AGL:

Depth	=	2000
Dir	=	171
Speed	=	1
Turb	=	0

Position Set:

Aircraft North	=	21371.378
East	=	6481.4524
Alt	=	377.8736
Heading	=	002

Buzzing by the Space Needle in Seattle was so much fun that you've decided to try it again—only this time at night. Are you crazy? Maybe. But it's a challenge you can't pass up.

As in the previous adventure, your starting point is the runway at Port Orchard, 16 miles west of Seattle. Except this time it's 10:30 p.m. instead of 10:30 a.m. Because it's dark, the simulator's map display will be an even more important navigational guide, so open it up and zoom it all the way out. As before, you want to look for the network of freeways—I-5, I-90, and State Route 520—that points the way to Seattle Center and the Space Needle. Remember that I-5 runs north/south along Puget Sound, and is intersected by I-90 and State Route 520 running east/west.

Soon after takeoff, make your turn to heading 030° well before the map display indicates that you're over the waters of Puget Sound. Level off at about 2500 feet.

Within a few minutes, the Sound will appear to be slipping beneath you. Mt. Rainier will be clearly visible on the horizon, thanks in part to the clear skies tonight; but the Space Needle is much more difficult to see. (It's almost like finding a needle in a haystack, you might say.) It appears first as a dim vertical line in the distance. When you spot it, make any course corrections that are necessary for a pass by its right side.

As you get closer, you'll see that the saucer-shaped observation and restaurant decks are ablaze with lights. Drop down to about 1000 feet for a closer look.

After you sweep by, bank into a steep left turn to circle back. This should put you on a heading of 230° or so, but again, it depends on your angle of approach and exactly when you made the earlier turn to 030°.

Of course, maneuvering at night is a bit more difficult than flying in the daytime. You have to rely more heavily on your instruments, particularly the altimeter, artificial horizon, and turn coordinator. Fortunately, the city lights surrounding Puget Sound brighten up the horizon, making it much easier to orient yourself when banking through turns. And the simulator's map display lets you cheat a little to keep track of your exact position, especially if you keep a road atlas handy (a recommended practice, incidentally).

Once again you're out over Puget Sound. And now—in case you were wondering—it's time for that same daredevil stunt you couldn't resist during the last flight. Sure—you're going to buzz right between the Space Needle's upper decks. Darkness be darned.

If you managed to pull it off last time, it will be a little easier now. And if you crashed, at least you'll know what *not* to do. So set yourself up by flying about halfway across Puget Sound, turning 180°, and descending to about 600 feet.

(Hint: To keep from losing the Space Needle in the darkness, it's a good idea to watch it from your back window while flying out over the Sound, then make your U-turn just before you lose sight of it. You can use the directional indicator—also known as the directional gyro or gyrocompass—to figure out the reciprocal of your current heading before making the U-turn. But first, make sure you've calibrated the directional indicator with the magnetic compass.)

After turning, line up your plane with the Needle early. As you'll recall from the previous flight, there won't be much time to fool around. And keep a watchful eye on that altimeter—a few feet too high, and you'll pass over the Needle; a few feet too low, and you risk splashing into the Sound or crashing into downtown Seattle.

Did you make it? If you did, congratulations! You deserve a gold star, and you're well on your way to becoming an expert simulator pilot.

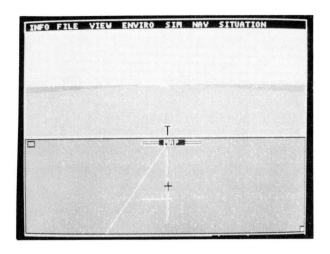

19
Sikorski's Dream

Environment: Summer
Time: 20:55:00
Carb Heat: On
Flaps: Up
Mags: Both
Lights: Off
Aircraft Orientation: On
Auto Coord: On
Sound: On

Winds:
Level 3 Tops = 7000
    Dir = 6
    Bot = 6000
    Speed = 23
    Turb = 0
Level 2 Tops = 6000
    Dir = 43

    Bot = 5000
    Speed = 12
    Turb = 0
Level 1 Tops = 5000
    Dir = 112
    Bot = 1000
    Speed = 9
    Turb = 0
Surface winds AGL:
    Depth = 1000
    Dir = 4
    Speed = 2
    Turb = 0
Position Set:
Aircraft North = 17551.000
    East = 21371.000
    Alt = 19.000
Heading = 026

A merica is a land made of dreams. Born from dreams of freedom and opportunity, this country has always attracted innovative, daring people. Igor Ivanovich Sikorski came to the United States with dreams of flight which he managed to make real. This Russian-born pioneer built one of the first single-rotor helicopters and built and piloted the first four-engine fixed-wing aircraft.

Your destination for this flight is Igor I. Sikorski Memorial Airport, just outside Stratford, Connecticut. Stratford lies east of Bridgeport on the banks of the Houstonic River and is a popular resort for at least two reasons: It's the home of both the American Shakespeare Theater and the National Helicopter Museum.

You'll be taking off from Hartford-Brainard Airport, in fair weather, early one summer morning. After you've completed the preflight check, set NAV-1 to 108.80. That's the frequency of the Bridgeport VOR, which you'll be using to navigate at the beginning of the flight. Plan to fly at a mean altitude of 4000 feet.

Give the plane full throttle, and take off. Your present heading is the reciprocal of the desired course heading shown by the VOR. To get on course, you need to make a 180-degree turn to head the plane in the opposite direction.

Gain some altitude. Now that you're off the ground, let's begin the gradual 180-degree turn. Cut the throttle down slightly; then bank left, recentering the aileron indicator shortly after you've begun to bank. The turn indicator should point to about two o'clock. Turn the plane gently, until it approaches a heading of 240°. When the compass gets to about 240°, start to bring the craft out of the turn with slight corrective banking to the right.

As you come out of the turn, try to attain the heading indicated by the VOR. Adjust the VOR knob if necessary to get the needle right on the center. Then get right on that radial and straighten out the craft.

Now perform some corrective measures. If you're not already at 4000 feet, get to that altitude and level out. Once that's done, lose a little speed, since there's no need to rush. Give the plane 10° of flaps. You'll see the airspeed indicator drop and gradually settle to a somewhat slower speed.

Snaking off into the distance is U.S. Highway 5, which runs right into New Haven, Connecticut, then merges with I-91 and I-95 on the way into Stratford. If you select the map display and zoom it out as far as possible, you can get a good view of the highway system as it leads to the coastline.

At about 35 miles from the Bridgeport VOR, you'll see an airport straight ahead. You know it's not your destination, since the instruments say you're still some 30 miles away. So, which airport is it? Study the charts. From the looks of things, it must be Chester, Tweed-New Haven, Meriden, or Waterbury-Oxford.

Use the automatic direction finder (ADF) to identify this airport by process of elimination. Tune the ADF to Waterbury-Oxford at 257. The needle points to the right. We know this airport isn't Waterbury-Oxford; if it were, the airport would appear to the right, too, rather than dead ahead. Now tune the ADF to Meriden NDB at 238. If you're still on course, the ADF needle should center exactly on the dial. The mystery airport is almost certainly Meriden.

You can tell for certain simply by waiting until you pass over the airport. This occurs when you're about 28 miles out from the Bridgeport VOR. If the ADF needle moves as you pass, it's Meriden. For an interesting view of the airport, look straight down as you pass overhead.

Meanwhile, the highway continues to meander along the coastline. Soon it's evident that the highway goes considerably farther than you want to go, if these instrument readings are correct. Speaking of instruments, it's time for another altitude check. Stay at about 4000 feet. If your heading has wandered off course, correct that as well.

Another airport becomes visible about 16 miles out of Bridgeport VOR. Is it Sikorski? Call the tower by tuning COM to 120.90. They're ready to receive you. The tower says runway 6. Take a downwind leg on your present heading; then make two 90-degree turns into the final approach.

Keep an eye on the VOR as you move over the airport. If the needle moves, you can confirm that this is Sikorski.

Look out the right-rear window as you pass the airport, and begin to orient yourself for the two 90-degree turns to the final approach. Fly the downwind leg until the airport is about to disappear from view in the right-rear window. (If you're well west of the airport you may need to use the direct rear view.) Then begin the turns and go in for a landing.

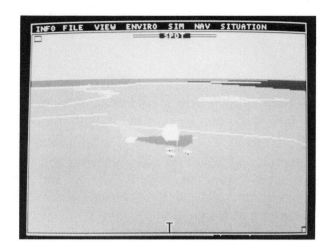

20
One If by Land

Environment: Spring
Time: 16:45:00
Carb Heat: On
Flaps: Up
Mags: Both
Lights: Off
Aircraft Orientation: On
Auto Coord: On
Sound: On

Winds:
Level 3 Tops	= No winds	
Level 2 Tops	= 5000	
Dir	= 26	
Bot	= 0	
Speed	= 12	
Turb	= 0	

Level 1 Tops = 6000
Dir = 112
Bot = 0
Speed = 9
Turb = None
Surface winds AGL:
Depth = 1000
Dir = 35
Speed = 3
Turb = 0
Position Set:
Aircraft North = 17868.000
East = 21833.000
Alt = 1706.000
Heading = 136

Special Instructions: Airspeed 119 knots

F or those who found the earlier flight to Boston fun, but frightening—here's another crack at landing at Boston's Logan Airport. In this adventure, we'll dispense with the preliminaries and start out in midair not far from the airport itself.

The simplest way to set up this midair situation is to take off from Oakland Airport (the default location) and gain the required airspeed and altitude. Level out the aircraft so that you're not gaining or losing altitude; then bring it around to exactly the right heading (136° in this case). Next, pause the program and use Position Set to put yourself at the right coordinates for the approach to Logan.

Once you're at the new position, set NAV-1 to 112.7 and COM to 119.10. Assume that you have already gotten clearance to land.

Next, pull down the Map display and zoom it all the way out for the largest possible view of the area. You won't have much time to survey the area before making your approach, and the map provides valuable orientation information. To avoid obscuring too much of the main view, keep the map tucked away in a corner of the main display window. Before you release the pause and take control, you may want to save the situation to disk for future use.

Remove the pause. You're cruising about 1700 feet above Boston. Below you is I-93. Off to the left, in the middle distance, is Logan Airport: You may just be able to make out two parallel runways. They are runways 22 right and 22 left. You'll be landing on runway 22 right, the larger of the two. Your VSI (Vertical Speed Indicator) should be at zero.

When Logan is about 90° off your left shoulder, begin a 90-degree turn to the left, to a heading of 40°. That's the reciprocal of the runway heading, meaning that when you come out of the turn, you'll be heading in exactly the opposite direction from the way you're going to land.

The plan is to maintain the reciprocal heading to the other side of the airport, then make two 90-degree turns to get lined up for the landing. The general term for all these maneuvers is the *approach*. More specifically, the reciprocal portion is called the *downwind* leg of the approach, and the portion after making the two 90-degree turns is called the *final* leg.

Go ahead and finish out the turn. Whenever you make a turn, you tend to lose a bit of altitude. That's not always bad—but in cases where you don't want to decrease altitude, pull the stick back slightly before you make the turn. This pulls the elevator down, generating just enough lift to keep your altitude constant during the turn. In later adventures, you'll try some turns that deliberately lose altitude. For now, just try to control it.

On most turns, you'll want to level out by moving the rudders and/or ailerons back to center about 10°–15° before you reach the desired heading. For example, if you're turning from a heading of 180° to a heading of 90°, you would start to come out of the turn at about 115°. If you're turning the other way, from a heading of 270° to 360°, you'd normally start to straighten out at about 345°. Once you get the feel of making turns, this anticipation becomes quite natural and intuitive, like the unconscious movements you make to straighten out a bicycle after turning it around a street corner.

After you level out from the first turn, you may be slightly off the optimum heading. If so, use a little bit of rudder to crab back onto just the right heading. Make sure that you haven't changed altitude too much. If you pulled back on the stick to maintain a constant altitude, push it back to its previous position to avoid gaining unwanted altitude. If you left the stick where it was throughout the turn, you should have lost no more than 200–300 feet.

At this point, you're flying the reciprocal, passing Logan on the left. You should be able to see the airport through your right window. After it leaves your right view, look back over your right shoulder. When Logan starts to appear in that window, it's time to make a 90-degree right turn, to a heading of 130°.

Your altitude should be no less than 1400 feet as you start the turn. In this one, go ahead and lose a bit of altitude, about 150 feet per minute. Start to come out of the turn at about 115°, pulling back on the yoke slightly.

Once level, you may be off heading again. If so, get back to 130°. Check your VSI once you've leveled out—are you rising or falling? Altitude control becomes more critical as you come closer to the ground. If you're still rising, stabilize your descent by taking off a little bit of throttle. After decreasing the throttle, you should also push down on the stick to raise your elevators and drop your vertical speed to a downward attitude. The ideal for this phase is a descent of about 150–250 feet per minute.

Look out the right window. If you haven't spent too much time getting straightened up, you should see Logan. If it's not in view, take advantage of the fact that you saved the beginning of the approach and start again.

Tune your VOR to the runway heading, 220°. Once the needle centers, Logan is just one 90-degree turn away. Use the same technique to continue in a controlled descent.

If everything has gone as planned, you should be between five and six miles from Boston VORTAC on the NAV-1 radio. Your altitude should be close to 1200 feet and your VSI should show that you're losing about 150–250 feet per minute.

It's time to slow down to a safe approach speed, using the flaps. If you lower the flaps 10°, you will lose some speed. Don't be alarmed if the VSI pops up temporarily. It should settle out fairly quickly. If it doesn't, correct the VSI by dropping the throttle a little more.

Now let's put this bird on the ground. Your most difficult task is to keep the aircraft straight on the runway heading. Don't lose your concentration—the closer you get to the ground, the less room you have to make mistakes. Begin by cutting down the throttle several notches. This causes the airplane to lose altitude. If you start to wander off the heading, correct it and push the flaps up one notch to slow your approach. Adjust the elevators up by pushing down on the stick.

When your altitude is about 100 feet, pull back on the stick to soften the impact. Watch your airspeed carefully as you approach the ground. If you get below 60 knots, the aircraft will start to stall. If necessary, you can exit the stall by increasing the throttle slightly and raising the flaps. (This may cause you to miss the runway, however.) As you approach terra firma, increase the lift on the elevators. The altitude at Logan is 20 feet. If you drop the throttle and lift the elevators just right, you'll settle onto the ground as softly as a falling feather.

You may or may not have attained the ideal of a feather-light landing. If you didn't, console yourself with the fact that landing with a flight simulator is much more difficult than putting a real aircraft down. As good as this program is, it still can't supply the full depth perception, peripheral vision, and all-important *seat of the pants* cues that guide a pilot in actual flight. On the other hand, one advantage of a simulator is that nobody cares how many times you meet the earth like a plummeting baby grand.

If this landing didn't meet your expectations, recall the saved situation and try it again. The practice will stand you in good stead when you move on to later adventures in this book.

21
The Power of the Pyramid

Environment: Winter
Time: 12:45:00
Carb Heat: Off
Flaps: Up
Mags: Both
Lights: Off
Aircraft Orientation: On
Auto Coord: On

Sound: On

Winds: None

Position Set:
Aircraft North = 17354.140
     East   = 5123.5733
     Alt   = 13.6240
Heading   = 277

s it truth, or just fancy, that pyramids possess a strange, compelling power? The crumbling, yet majestic, wonders of the ancient world at Giza have fascinated people for centuries. Were the Great Pyramids really built by thousands of laborers without sophisticated tools or machinery? If so, how were such massive structures erected with such unerring precision? Why were they built in the shape of pyramids? Are they really just elaborate tombs and nothing more?

Questions such as these are buzzing through your head as you warm up your plane just off runway 29 at Oakland International Airport. Today you're going to fly right by a pyramid for a close-up look with your own eyes, searching for a flash of insight that may answer some of your questions.

Of course, you can't make it from California to Egypt on a single tank of gas (not unless you're flying the *Voyager*). Instead, the pyramid you're going to inspect is across the bay in San Francisco—the well-known Transamerica building. You've seen it in pictures, on television, and in movies. Now you want to see what it looks like from the air.

The Transamerica pyramid affords us a modern-day chance to explore the mysteries of the past. Even after 4500 years, we aren't so advanced that cultural icons and images don't hold a special meaning or magnetism for us, just as they did for the ancients. The Transamerica pyramid became an instant classic as soon as it was finished, a West Coast counterpart to the Empire State Building. It proves that some things never go out of style.

Complete your preflight checks, tuning in the Oakland ILS (Instrument Landing System) on NAV-1 at frequency 108.7. Tune in the tower at 128.5 on the COM radio, and—for cross-reference—the Oakland VORTAC at 116.8 on NAV-2.

Taxi onto runway 29, line up on a heading of 294°, and take off. As soon as you're off the ground, look backward. Some of the most beautiful runways in the simulation are at

Oakland, and the south strips are particularly detailed and realistic. Much more detail than this, and you'd have to fasten seat belts.

Soon after takeoff you'll hear the the marker beeps for the Oakland ILS (though on the Macintosh you'll only see the indicator lights). Return to the front view and level off at a cruising altitude of 2500 feet. Just ahead you'll see the San Francisco–Oakland Bay Bridge, a marvelous structure itself. Moments later the city of San Francisco comes into view. In the distance, you can clearly see the Golden Gate Bridge, which connects San Francisco to Marin County.

Steer left and aim straight for the middle of the Golden Gate Bridge. Gradually descend to 500 feet in preparation for your sightseeing mission. After a minute or two you'll pass right between the pylons of the bridge, but your altitude should be sufficient to avoid an embarrassing collision. Tip your wings at the people below to show them you're a polite pilot.

Leveled off at 500 feet, you'll be able to get a good look at the scenery. Just don't forget how low you are during the upcoming maneuvers. The plane responds a bit sluggishly at low altitudes, so you'll have to be more attentive than usual when making turns.

After passing over the Golden Gate Bridge, start a left turn. This turn may require a few notches of up-elevator to keep from losing altitude. (When the turn is complete, re-adjust the elevators to maintain at 500 feet.) Don't come out of the turn until you can see the San Francisco skyline dead ahead, even if it seems you've turned all the way around. Fly straight toward the crowded skyline until you can pick out your target from among the other towers overlooking the Bay. You shouldn't have any trouble distinguishing it, because it's recognizably a pyramid even from a distance of a couple of miles.

Continue flying straight toward the Transamerica building for a good, close look. Be careful not to hit it, of course.

As you zip by, a crazy thought pops into your head. Wouldn't it be great to land right next to the pyramid and taxi around it for a *really* good view? Well, why not? There's probably plenty of room on the street down there. And just think of the midday boredom you'll relieve for all of the office workers.

Give it a try. Keep flying on your present course for a minute or two, watching the pyramid from your rear window. When it seems to lose its recognizable shape, make a U-turn. (Watch out for the Oakland Bay Bridge; depending on your angle of approach, you may come close to hitting it.) Slow down the aircraft, being very careful to maintain your low altitude.

It may help to imagine that there's a runway alongside the building—or even that the building sits in the middle of an airport with dozens of crisscross runways. This is one of the more curious features about *Flight Simulator*. For all its realism, it's still a fallible computer program. Because it's an incomplete simulation of the real world, you can perform feats of daring that otherwise would be quite impossible. Some people regard this as a limitation; others, as an advantage. Although it might be nice to have a simulation that recreates every street, building, and sidewalk, a simulation that real would, by nature, limit you to the same actions that are feasible in real life. And real life, as we all know, is sometimes boring. An undeniable attraction of the simulator is its potential for escapism.

So to make your outlandish landing, aim right toward the green area surrounding the pyramid. Put the plane down as close as you can; then taxi over from wherever you stop. Be careful, though—the simulator isn't completely fallible. Once on the ground, you can taxi into a building and wreck your plane.

One missing element from the simulator is that you can't look straight up at the building. This is too bad, because the Transamerica pyramid offers a strange and exciting optical illusion to observers on the ground. It's a sight that shouldn't be missed by anyone who visits San Francisco.

The optical illusion works like this: Our eyes are accustomed to perceiving converging lines as evidence of perspective and distance. That is, if you look upward at a conventional skyscraper, the converging lines of its parallel sides give you a visual clue as to how tall the building is. But the Transamerica pyramid fools the eyes, because its sloping sides do, in fact, converge toward a point. Therefore, if you stand on a certain spot on the sidewalk and look straight up at it, the building appears to be much, much taller than it really is. Indeed, it seems to touch the sky. And like all optical illusions, it helps if you play along with the deception and try to forget what you're really looking at.

Anyway, after you've looked around a little, it's time to fly back to Oakland. Taxi the aircraft until it is aimed in the general direction of the Oakland Bay Bridge. (If you can't see it from the ground, open up the map display and zoom in as required. Don't confuse it with the Golden Gate Bridge.) Take off and climb quickly to about 1000 feet.

To get on course, steer toward the Oakland Bay Bridge and fly directly over the length of it. In other words, fly as if you're on the bridge's upper deck. Your heading while you're following the bridge will be roughly 030°. Keep your altitude at about 1000 feet so you can see the bridge at all times.

When you reach the end of the bridge, make a quick right turn to heading 120°. You are now on the downwind for Oakland International Airport. Call the tower to confirm, and bring her down. After your daring stunt in downtown San Francisco, this landing should be a cinch.

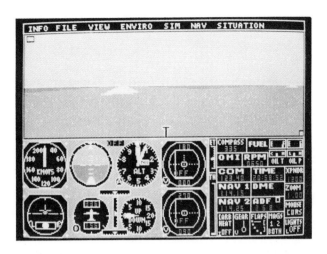

22
The House That Ruth Built

Environment: Summer
Time: 20:55:00
Carb Heat: On
Flaps: On
Mags: Both
Lights: Off
Aircraft Orientation: On
Auto Coord: On
Sound: On

Winds:

Level 3 Tops	=	No wind
Level 2 Tops	=	5000
Dir	=	110
Bot	=	4000
Speed	=	5

Turb	=	0
Level 1 Tops	=	4000
Dir	=	110
Bot	=	1000
Speed	=	4
Turb	=	0

Surface winds AGL:

Depth	=	1000
Dir	=	110
Speed	=	3
Turb	=	0

Position Set:

Aircraft North	=	17089.000
East	=	21177.000
Alt	=	81.000
Heading	=	322

L et's examine this island a little further. There are several land-marks of interest. This is Republic Airport, just east of Farmingdale, New York, on Long Island. Make your preflight check; then tune in La Guardia VOR at 113.1. The VOR needle should center at about 292. As soon as you're airborne, you can fly on that radial to Manhattan Island.

Go ahead and take off. Apply your brakes, give the plane full throttle, and at 2450 rpm, release the brakes. Pull the stick back when your speed reaches about 60 knots.

Climb to 2000 feet; then drop the throttle slightly. The object is to level off at about 2500 feet. Now re-adjust the VOR, because it will be moving as you fly away from the airport. Turn several degrees to the left so that your heading matches the VOR reading.

La Guardia is now straight ahead. Fly directly over it. While you're sightseeing, do some work with altitude control. Keeping a steady altitude requires a balance between the elevators and the throttle. The VSI tells you whether or not you've attained steady, level flight—neither climbing nor dropping. Try descending to 1000 feet. Drop the nose of the craft to begin the descent. Watch the altimeter. As it gets closer to 1000 feet, drop the throttle until the rpm needle settles right around 1950. Then adjust the elevators as needed—pulling back or pushing forward gently on the stick—until the VSI needle centers at zero. If you have a lot of trouble stabilizing the plane, try getting the engine down to 1850 rpm. Keep working until you get it right.

Back to the sightseeing tour. La Guardia becomes clearly visible as an airport at a distance of 10 to 12 miles. From about 3½ miles out of La Guardia, the cityscape behind the airport begins to emerge as a darker area of land crisscrossed by light motorways. When you are directly above La Guardia, several tall buildings should be visible in your left-front view. The right-rear view should be mostly water. Beyond the two bridges, which connect Queens and the Bronx, is Long Island Sound.

After you've crossed the water and come over Manhattan, Central Park is clearly visible as a long rectangular area located smack-dab in the middle of the island. When Central Park is nearly off your left wing, make a left turn to about 230° and fly over the park as though you're going to land there. Come down to an altitude of about 400 feet by cutting the throttle to 1350, giving the plane 2° of flaps, and lowering the elevators. When the plane reaches 500 feet, pull back slightly on the elevators to level off.

Now you're ready for a dazzling view of the Big Apple. That's the Empire State Building on your left. Watch it out the left window as you go by. You may have to increase the throttle just a bit to avoid landing on Wall Street. The altitude of Manhattan is pretty close to sea level, so don't let the altimeter slip below 200 feet.

Next up are the World Trade Center towers. You're going to fly right between them. It may not look possible from a distance, but you can actually do it with room to spare. This maneuver is done entirely on visual orientation. Watch your altitude: It's fairly easy to crash into the ground while your attention is focused on threading the needle between these two behemoths. Don't lose heart at the last moment. If your heading is something around 225° and your center orientation lies equidistant between the two buildings, you'll glide through without a scratch, even though it looks as if you're about to lose both wings.

If you just entered one of the World Trade Center towers from the air, don't worry about it. One of the beauties of a flight simulator is that it allows you to try things that would land you in jail, or the hospital—or both—in real life. At worst, you'll have to start the flight over again. If you're the cautious type, you can always save the current situation to RAM before you attempt a daring maneuver. That way, if you crash, you don't have to start over from the very beginning of the flight.

If you're still in the air, the body of water before you is Upper New York Bay. Manhattan Island juts out into the bay. Follow the end of the island around to the left. As you make the turn, remember that banking causes you to lose altitude somewhat. To compensate for the loss, pull back on the stick before you start the turn and return the elevators to the previous setting as you come out of it.

Stay out over the water and keep turning until the bay narrows into a river. This is a pretty sharp turn. The southwestern tip of Manhattan, where the World Trade Center lies, comes to a sharp point, almost like a pencil.

Below you is the East River. Dead ahead is the famous Brooklyn Bridge—an engineering marvel in its day and still a grand sight. Next you'll see a highway crossing the river. Keep following the river as it winds around Manhattan. Off to your right is the borough of Queens.

Another highway crosses the river. Stay over the water. The river narrows soon and eventually comes to a sort of unruly T-junction. If you zoom out the right-front view, you can see La Guardia Airport again. Just before the river gives out altogether, turn left about 45°. In the real world, this would be where the Harlem River runs north, separating the Bronx from Manhattan. Harlem River Drive runs along the river to your left, and the Major Deegan Expressway borders it to your right. A short way up the river, not far beyond the Expressway, is the site of old Yankee Stadium, "The House That Ruth Built."

But you won't see Ruth's house on this flight, except in your imagination. There are limits to every simulation, and you just reached the end of the details in this particular cityscape.

Since I've led you from reality into limbo, it's fitting that this adventure end in no particular way. You can circle the Bronx a few times, if you like, just to scope things out. Who knows—perhaps you really will spot Yankee Stadium, and circle low just as a ball, hit impossibly high, flies up to greet your craft amidst the clouds. It wouldn't be the first time that a dream came true in this town.

On the other hand, you may be interested in returning to Earth at some point. One option is to retrace your steps back to Republic and land whence you came. Or, you could turn around and find your way to the ground at La Guardia. Or, you may want to point the plane at the Atlantic and fly straight ahead until darkness, and dreams, envelop you.

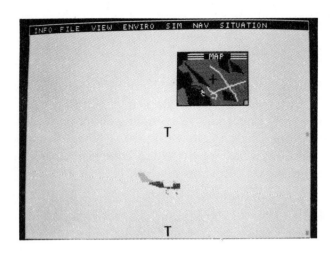

23
Dove Descending

Environment: Fall
Time: 15:20:00
Carb Heat: Off
Flaps: Up
Mags: Both
Lights: Off
Aircraft Orientation: On
Auto Coord: On
Sound: On

Winds:
Level 3 Tops	=	6000
Dir	=	124
Bot	=	3000
Speed	=	3
Turb	=	0
Level 2 Tops	=	3000
Dir	=	34
Bot	=	1500
Speed	=	3
Turb	=	0
Level 1 Tops	=	1500

Dir	=	60
Bot	=	1000
Speed	=	5
Turb	=	0

Surface winds AGL:
Depth	=	1000
Dir	=	34
Speed	=	2
Turb	=	0

Position Set:
Aircraft North	=	17368.027
East	=	5174.0234
Alt	=	4500.0000
Heading	=	59

Clouds:
Level 1 Tops	=	20000
Base	=	1500
Level 2	=	None
Ground Fog	=	None

F or this short adventure, you start out 4500 feet above Alameda County in the San Francisco Bay Area. You're not up to anything particularly important—just tooling along on a recreational flight to see the Golden Gate Bridge. Yes, it's a cloudy day, but fortunately the base of the cloud cover is just high enough (1500 feet) that you can drop beneath it for a good view.

Now here's the rub. At the Alameda Naval Air Station, Treasure Island Naval Air Station, Nimitz Field, and the numerous other bases around San Francisco Bay, the military is conducting an extensive exercise and has warned all private aircraft within ten nautical miles to stay above 5000 feet. Since you don't want to tangle with an F-14 Tomcat or an F/A-18 Hornet in your single-engine Cessna, you're only too willing to cooperate. This means you'll have to stay in the clouds until you get well past Nimitz Field, and then descend below the clouds to take a peek at the bridge.

But how will you know when to descend if you're flying blind in the clouds? You'll use your instruments, of course—specifically, the OBI, VOR, DME, and NAV radio.

To get started, look at your San Francisco area chart to find the nearest VOR station to the Golden Gate Bridge. This happens to be Sausalito in Marin County, which the bridge links with San Francisco. Tune in the Sausalito VOR on NAV-1 at 116.2 and check the DME. It shows that you're about 24 miles out.

Next, center the OBI needle and turn to the indicated heading to fly toward Sausalito. Your compass heading will be in the 250°–260° range, but you'll probably need to recalibrate after your turn to get a more exact heading.

Finally, don't forget to climb above 5000 feet so you're not mistaken for an intruding MiG in the military exercises.

(Incidentally, you may notice that the instruments are slightly more sensitive in cloudy or less-than-fair weather. This isn't typical of real planes, so regard it as a gift from Mr. Artwick—a freak of simulation nature, if you will.)

When the DME indicates you're about 12 miles out, there's another decision to be made. Looking at the chart, you can see that Sausalito lies just north of the Golden Gate. To see the bridge, you need to descend somewhere south of the Sausalito VOR. Just how far south can't be determined under these conditions and with these instruments. So you make a guesstimate: Fly about 20° south of the VOR. Subtract 20° from the heading indicated on the OBI, and turn to that radial.

Watch your altitude. Don't stay too much above 5000 feet, because it will be difficult to drop below the cloud cover when the moment arrives. A cruising altitude of about 5200 feet is fine.

When the DME indicates that you're six miles from Sausalito, begin your descent. This will be a fairly steep dive—aim for 1500 feet per minute on the VSI. If you don't lose altitude fast enough, you'll miss the bridge. Of course, if you get carried away and lose altitude *too* fast, you'll take a swim in San Francisco Bay. And the Bay has been known to contain sharks.

Keep an eye on the DME, too. At first it indicates that you're closing fast on Sausalito, but then it slows down. Soon it reverses and starts increasing. Remember that you aren't flying directly toward Sausalito anymore.

As soon as the altimeter hits 1500, you pop out of the clouds and the spectacular Bay Area scenery suddenly comes into view. If everything went according to plan, you should see the Golden Gate Bridge directly in front of and beneath you. Cruise by for a good look, and wave at the joggers.

If you can't see the bridge, you probably didn't descend quite fast enough, and overshot the target. If the front view reveals nothing but water, switch to your back view. See it now? Either circle back for a look, or repeat the flight from scratch to hone your cloudy-weather flying skills.

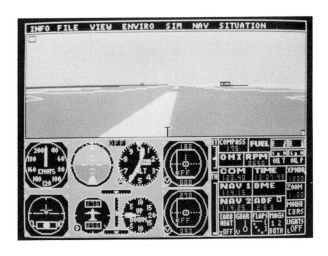

24
The Meigs Factor

Environment: Fall
Time: 13:04:00
Carb Heat: On
Flaps: Up
Mags: Both
Lights: Off
Aircraft Orientation: On
Auto Coord: On
Sound: On

Winds:

Level 3 Tops	=	9000
Dir	=	330
Bot	=	6000
Speed	=	5
Turb	=	0
Level 2 Tops	=	6000
Dir	=	345
Bot	=	3000
Speed	=	6
Turb	=	0
Level 1 Tops	=	3000
Dir	=	318
Bot	=	1000
Speed	=	5
Turb	=	0

Surface winds AGL:

Depth	=	1000
Dir	=	285
Speed	=	4
Turb	=	0

Position Set:

Aircraft North	=	17189.776
East	=	16670.959
Alt	=	597.000
Heading	=	178

W hat a beautiful autumn day! You're about to take a pleasure flight from Chicago's Merrill C. Meigs Airport. You'll be going to Lansing Municipal, which is very close to the Illinois/Indiana border. Tune NAV-1 to 114.2, the Chicago Heights VOR frequency.

You'll be carrying a somewhat peculiar passenger. You don't usually take passengers on such short notice, but it's a short flight and he agreed to pay extra for the inconvenience. His three heavy duffle bags have already been stowed and secured for takeoff. When you climb into the cockpit, you notice that he's sweating, even though the fall weather is cool and he's lightly dressed.

Perhaps he's never been in a plane before, you think to yourself. As you begin the preflight check, you decide to reassure your passenger with some innocuous conversation. Who wants to fly to Lansing with somebody who looks like he's ready to chew his way through the windshield?

"I've made this flight dozens of times before," you begin. "It's a short, easy flight for an experienced pilot."

"Yes, I'm sure," he replies.

"Of course, it may not seem so routine to someone who's not used to flying. Have you ever been in an airplane before?"

"Oh yes, many times."

Sure you have, you think. *And I'll be made a national hero for hauling this bozo and his duffle from Meigs to Lansing Muni. This guy hasn't been off the ground since he wore three-cornered pants and bounced on his daddy's knee.*

At least the pay is right. As you complete the preflight check, you notice that your passenger hasn't been able to sit still since he got into the aircraft. Time to get off the ground. As you begin to taxi down the runway, you notice him craning his neck to the left.

"That's Lake Michigan to the left of us," you point out. "To the front of us, too, for that matter." When you think about it, you recall that Meigs was an unsettling place for you to fly out of the first time, too. So little land, surrounded by so much water. Not that it makes much difference which one you hit if you're going, say, 90 knots. But the land always seems safer.

You've just left the ground and are gaining altitude. Now your passenger is looking wildly out the window on his side. Water, water, everywhere.

Maybe it really is time to calm this guy down, you think. Even nervous passengers usually settle down somewhat once you reach altitude and the craft stops bouncing around.

"We'll reach our cruising altitude soon," you say in a calming voice as you set the VOR for Chicago Heights. "This instrument helps us stay on the right course. We're already going in the right direction, so if we just keep on doing what we're doing, you should be able to see the Lansing airport in just a few minutes."

He nods with a rigid motion. The plane has reached about 2000 feet and then levels off. It banks slightly as you make a small course correction. Then the craft settles into straight, level flight. This flight may not end in disaster, after all.

Suddenly, your radio crackles with a message from the Meigs tower. Your passenger cocks his head to listen, but can't really follow it—something about Zulus and niners. There's a lot of static, and these airplane people seem to speak their own peculiar lingo, anyway.

You say something to the tower, then switch to a different frequency and plug in a headset to listen. Unbeknownst to your passenger, here's what the tower says:

Repeat, the guy you have on board either is a terrorist or belongs in a rubber room. Information we have is that he's carrying three bags of plastic explosive and other toys. Suspected of planting a bomb in a downtown hotel so his buddies could hold it for ransom. Return to Meigs at once and do not alarm him.

"We have to change course," you say, as you bank the plane back toward Meigs. "The control tower noticed some strange-looking smoke coming from the engine when we took off. Probably nothing serious, but there's no reason to take chances. You can probably hire another plane within the hour."

But another hour might be too late. The man glances wildly about the plane as it resumes course for Meigs. You eye him carefully. When he grabs for something inside his coat, you knock him out with a single, right-handed jab to the temple. Looks like you might become a hero after all—if you can just land this crate at Meigs before he wakes up. Break a leg.

25
Fable de Saible

Environment: Spring
Time: 09:00:00
Carb Heat: Off
Flaps: Up
Mags: Both
Lights: Off
Aircraft Orientation: On
Auto Coord: On
Sound: On

Winds:
Level 3 Tops = No winds
Level 2 Tops = 7000
    Dir = 280
    Bot = 2000
    Speed = 5

    Turb = 1
Level 1 Tops = 2000
    Dir = 260
    Bot = 1000
    Speed = 6
    Turb = 0
Surface winds AGL:
    Depth = 1000
    Dir = 190
    Speed = 2
    Turb = 0
Position Set:
Aircraft North = 16471.000
    East = 16685.000
    Alt = 699.000
Heading = 048

According to the history books, a fur trader from Haiti—Jean Baptiste Point de Saible—built the first house on the site of what is now Chicago. That was in 1779. De Saible didn't follow the paths of earlier French explorers, however. Rather than arriving via the rivers and Great Lakes, de Saible traveled across what is now Indiana. In this adventure, you'll approximately retrace his path, but in a way he could only have dreamed of—through the air.

After taking off from Vermilion County Airport, Illinois, a few miles from the Indiana state line, you'll travel to the small airfield at Lewis University near Chicago. Along the way, you'll get some practice flying in light turbulence and make your first landing at a single-strip airport.

After your normal preflight check, make a normal takeoff on runway 4 (compass heading 048°). There are light winds today and some turbulence at the middle altitudes, but nothing that should interfere with your takeoff.

Immediately after leaving the ground and starting your climb to a cruising altitude of 3000 feet, you see fields of crops appearing on the horizon. At around 2700 feet, you encounter just enough turbulence to make your piloting job interesting.

Tune in NAV-1 to Danville, Illinois, at 111.0. Depending on how quickly you've reached cruising altitude, you may have already passed the Danville VOR. This will become apparent when you calibrate your OBI—if it reads FROM instead of TO, you've left it behind. In any event, change course to this new heading. It should be roughly 013°.

The next VOR is Joliet at 112.3. It's quite a distance away yet, so if you don't get a reading from the DME, you're probably out of range. Be patient. You'll pick it up when you're about 80 miles out. When it comes in, recalibrate and fly toward it at the indicated heading, which should be around 325°.

If you're having a little trouble handling the turbulence, don't feel bad. The turbulence factors in the Macintosh, ST, and Amiga versions of the flight simulator are a trifle tougher than in versions for other computers—perhaps a consequence of the faster execution speeds. Just keep an eye on the compass heading so you don't wander too far off course.

The scenery is fairly plain in this region. De Saible must have thought he'd reached the outer limits when he came through here more than 200 years ago. But for a fur trapper, it was paradise. The virgin woods abounded with rabbit, bear, deer, and sable—the highly prized animals from which de Saible may have adopted his surname.

Pretty soon something comes into view on the horizon. An Indian village, perhaps? Several large villages existed in this area in de Saible's time, and he must have enjoyed tolerable relations with the Indians to carry on his successful fur-trapping business. In fact, it's said that de Saible even married a local Indian woman. Maybe that's how he escaped the fate later suffered by the army garrison at Fort Dearborn—established near his house on the site of modern-day downtown Chicago—which was burned in 1812.

Back to the twentieth century. The image now clarifying on the horizon isn't an Indian village after all, but a body of water. As de Saible himself almost certainly would have done, you're going to take a slight detour to see where the water leads.

Soon you see a large black area near the water. This is the city of Kankakee, Illinois. The Kankakee River flows north from here until it merges with the Illinois River, which eventually becomes the Chicago River. The Chicago River empties into Lake Michigan at the site of Fort Dearborn, which today is outlined by metal plaques embedded in the sidewalks along Michigan Avenue.

After passing over Kankakee, keep following the river. This will force you to stray a bit from your VOR heading, so change course to approximately 308°.

In the simulator, the Kankakee River flows to an abrupt dead end before it reaches Chicago. But assuming that this is where the Kankakee meets the Illinois, turn northeast to a heading of about 005° to continue following its imaginary course. In a moment, this will take you over Joliet, whose VOR you're still tracking.

About 20 miles out, Joliet should come into view. At a range of about 17 miles, the deep blue waters of Lake Michigan should become visible on the horizon toward your right. (You may have to switch to the simulator's front-right view for a glimpse of the lake.) And in another minute or two, you should see I-55 snaking just beyond Joliet.

Between the city of Joliet and I-55 is a small airport—Lewis University. Its single east/west runway should become visible as you approach Joilet. Your left view should reveal another airport, Joliet Park. And out of your right or right-front window, you may see one or two more airports—New Lenox-Howell and Frankfort. As you'll discover in a moment, simply finding the right airport in this crowded metropolitan corridor is a major job in itself.

Since Lewis University is your target, a few course changes are required to get on runway heading into the wind.

As you're passing over the city of Joliet, make a right turn to heading 020°. This steers you in a general direction toward Lake Michigan in order to give you some room to maneuver.

Keep checking your ground view to see when you've passed completely over Joliet. Then bank fairly sharply to a new heading of 090°. This aims your plane due east on a downwind leg. You probably see some airports directly ahead—New Lenox-Howell, or Frankfort, or Crestwood Howell, or perhaps all three. Try to ignore these distractions. It's not hard to land at the wrong airport in this area.

Check your tail view to keep an eye on the city of Joliet, which should be receding in the distance. When the outlines of the entire city are visible near the center of your window, bank fairly sharply again to a heading of 000°—due north.

Now check your left window. Joliet and I-55 should be in view near the horizon, with the Lewis University airstrip midway between.

Keep watching your left window. If you've made these tricky turns exactly right, your plane should be just south of the single east/west Lewis runway. Just before you draw even with the runway (remember, you're looking west), turn quickly to your final runway heading of 270°. This aims your plane due west, approximately into the wind, and aligns you with the Lewis runway.

Your front view should now reveal Lewis dead ahead. If you're lucky, your plane is lined up for a perfect landing. If not, make some minor course corrections for your final approach.

There's not much runway here, so don't wait too long to lose altitude. Otherwise, you'll fly right over the runway and have to try again.

Did you make it down safely? If so, check your position to confirm that you've landed at the right airport. (Lewis's co-ordinates should be approximately 17081 north and 16518 east.)

If your coordinates are radically different, you evidently made a wrong turn somewhere and got lost. You may console yourself that Jean Baptiste Point de Saible probably got lost in these parts, too. But then, de Saible didn't have the advantage of an aerial view, a VOR beacon, and a zoom map display. What's your excuse?

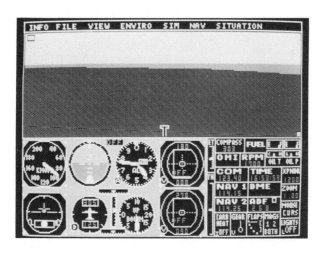

26
Howdy, Pilgrim

Environment: Spring
Time: 16:53:00
Carb Heat: Off
Flaps: Up
Mags: Both
Lights: Off
Aircraft Orientation: On
Auto Coord: On
Sound: On

Winds:

Level 3 Tops	=	3995
Dir	=	118
Bot	=	2995
Speed	=	7
Turb	=	0
Level 2 Tops	=	2995
Dir	=	118

Bot	=	1995
Speed	=	7
Turb	=	0
Level 1 Tops	=	1995
Dir	=	117
Bot	=	495
Speed	=	5
Turb	=	0
Surface winds AGL:		
Depth	=	495
Dir	=	116
Speed	=	14
Turb	=	0
Position Set:		
Aircraft North	=	15343.000
East	=	5643.0000
Alt	=	5304.0000
Heading	=	300

Howdy, Pilgrim. Your destination on this flight is an airport in Southern California named after The Duke himself— John Wayne. Located in Orange County between Santa Ana and Irvine, John Wayne Airport is near the Costa Mesa Freeway and Upper Newport Bay.

Actually, John Wayne wasn't your original destination. You were headed for Los Angeles International, but the LAX tower redirected you to Orange County because of congested air traffic. So when the adventure starts, you'll find yourself 5300 feet over the Pacific Ocean, heading away from John Wayne. If you check your rear view, you'll see Santa Catalina Island directly behind you and the Southern California coastline on your right.

First, tune in your NAV-1 radio to John Wayne at 109.40. When you adjust the VOR needle accordingly, you'll see that you're considerably off course from your new destination. The instrument reports that your heading should be about 083°.

Before steering toward John Wayne, however, you decide that since you're taking a detour anyway, you might as well do some sightseeing in the meantime. You make up your mind to take a peek at Santa Catalina Island.

Bank into a fairly steep right turn to reach a heading of about 130°. This should aim you straight toward Santa Catalina, with the mainland on your left.

It will take you several minutes to reach the island. As you come nearer, you'll notice a white speck near its eastern tip. That's an airport. It's a fairly large strip with CT radios and VOR. It's private, though, so if you ever want to land there, you have to get permission first.

The Catalina runway is on a heading of 040°. If you're on course, you should be just to the west of the airstrip. Stick to your current course of 130° and open your map view. Zoom it out for the minimum magnification. It should show most or all of Santa Catalina Island and the airstrip. At the same time, recalibrate your VOR needle for a corrected heading to John Wayne. It should read approximately 045°.

When the map view shows that you're passing directly over the Catalina airport, turn left to the new VOR heading. This should aim you straight for the mainland, and the megalopolis of Los Angeles should appear as a large gray patch along the coastline.

About 20 miles out, the Santa Ana Mountains come into view on the horizon, and the San Diego Freeway stretches across the full width of your screen. Between the freeway and the coastline, you'll soon see a white speck—John Wayne Airport.

Time to tune in to the tower. Set your COM radio to 126.00. John Wayne ATIS reports ten-mile visibility; wind, 116 at 14 knots; and runway 19, the strip of choice.

One more turn should do it. If you closed your map view, reopen it and make sure it's zoomed out for minimum magnification. When you're almost over land, bank right to parallel the coastline and start losing altitude. Without delay, check your left-front view. Watch until the runways at John Wayne are nearly lined up with your left wing; then quickly bank left to make your final approach.

Hopefully you encountered no problems and made a smooth landing. Taxi around to the terminal, again checking the map view to find your way if necessary.

But the adventure isn't over yet. While your plane is being serviced, some people approach and ask if you'll fly them to Ontario International Airport in Ontario, California. In return, they offer you a videotape of *The Man Who Shot Liberty Valance*, a classic flick starring Jimmy Stewart and—who else?—John Wayne. This is the movie that popularized Wayne's slogan, "Howdy, Pilgrim." You can't resist the offer.

After checking over your freshened-up plane, you get clearance to take off from runway 01. You waste no time climbing to an altitude of 2500 feet.

As soon as you're off the ground at John Wayne, tune in your NAV-1 to Pomona at 110.4. Adjust the VOR needle; it should show Pomona on a heading of approximately 355°. Turn to this new heading and level out at an altitude of about

3500 feet. Your plan is to fly toward Pomona, tune in Swan Lake on your ADF (at 257), and wait until Swan Lake is about 90° from your position. Then you'll catch Ontario on visual and make a right turn to intercept the downwind pattern for runway 26.

As you're cruising along, you'll get a good view of the Santa Ana Mountains from your right window. And in a few minutes, the San Gabriel Mountains pop into view straight ahead. Luckily you won't have to fly over them today; Ontario is in the foothills. Also in view are several of the ever-present LA-area freeways: probably the Orange Freeway, Pomona Freeway, San Bernardino Freeway, and the Colorado Freeway. Aren't you glad you're not commuting today?

Very shortly you'll be able to see an airport between two of the freeways: Bracket Field at Pomona. Check your right and right-front views in search of Ontario; you can't see it. But re-lax—you know it's there, and it's almost time to make your turn.

You'll know instantly when you pass over Bracket Field; the Pomona VOR needle will fluctuate wildly from TO to OFF to FROM. Immediately check the ADF. When it shows that Swan Lake is 90° from your current course, bank right to a new heading of 080°.

Before too long, another airport pops into view straight ahead. Is it Ontario? Doesn't look large enough. Might be Chino Airport. Be patient for another minute or two.

Finally, Ontario is visible just to the left of Chino. Adjust your heading, if necessary, so you're flying right between the two airports—Ontario on the left, and Chino on the right. Your passengers compliment you on your flawless navigation. "It was nothin'," you quip, glancing at them from behind your mirrored sunglasses.

You are downwind from the pattern at Ontario, so fly by the airport at an altitude of about 3000 feet. Watch Ontario slide across your left window as you pass by. The advantage of entering patterns is clear: Traffic is kept controlled and organized; no plane is allowed to interfere with another. All aircraft are given enough time to adjust and correct their angle of attack, altitude, and airspeed for a well-executed, safe landing.

Just before Ontario slides out of view from your left-rear window, turn left 90° to a heading of approximately 000°. Then watch the airport out of your left windows until you're lined up, and turn left into the final approach. Keep in mind that the altitude here, in the foothills of the San Gabriels, is just under 1000 feet.

Safely on the ground—and with the precious videotape in hand—you bid your passengers goodbye and begin checking the plane for the return trip to John Wayne. Reopen the map view if you closed it, and see how well you lined up on the runway.

The return flight is pretty straightforward. Taxi up to the intercepting runway at Ontario and take off. As soon as you're in the air, tune in the John Wayne VOR at 109.4, and come to the indicated heading. You're about 25 miles away, and the flight will go fast.

Before you know it, Santa Ana becomes visible again. When it does, turn right about 20° from the VOR heading. You should fly just north (to the right, from your point of view) of John Wayne.

Intercept the traffic pattern on the downwind. Take a good look at John Wayne; it should be familiar to you now. Remember that there's a small runway just beyond the terminal that you'll be aiming for. If you missed it last time, here's your second chance.

Check your views, make your turn, and line up with the small runway in the middle. Since you've already made two landings today, this one should be old hat—a white hat, of course—right, pilgrim?

27
How High
Is the Sky?

Note: There are no parameters to enter for this adventure. Simply boot up the simulator and get ready to take off. Select the Learjet 25G for this adventure.

This adventure is a benchmark. It's the only one in this book which starts at the default location (runway 27R at Oakland Airport).

What you'll benchmark today is the jet's altitude ceiling. Here's how the test will work. You'll fly the Learjet in minute patterns, ascending while you make a 90-degree turn every seven minutes. The effect will be to square the airport over and over as you rise at the jet's maximum climb speed. At some point in the flight, the jet will stop climbing, and you'll know you've reached maximum altitude. If you're the cautious type, you may want to request an oxygen tank at the airport's supply station.

When you've performed the preflight checks, it's time to buckle up and go. To make the test more authentic, be sure to raise the landing gear after takeoff.

Once in the air, your job is to attain the highest constant climb rate on the VSI. It's best to use the keyboard rather than the mouse or joystick for this particular adjustment. With the throttle at maximum, move the elevators up (pull back on the stick) gradually until the jet just begins to stall. When it does, lower the elevators gradually, one notch at a time, until you recover from the stall. Remember the number of notches you just lowered the elevators. If the plane stalls again, repeat the process with one more notch of adjustment. It's important for this test to be sure that you have the highest possible vertical speed.

When you arrive at the maximum climb speed, make a note of it. The VSI readings are on the meter on your control panel and are read in hundreds of feet per minute.

Now it's time to start the minute patterns. Look at the clock and write down the time. Then look out the back window to gauge your distance from the airport. If it's still clearly in sight, you're ready to begin. If not, turn around and fly back until it's in sight. If you have to find the airport again, note how many minutes you flew before you began the patterns. At the end of the test you'll subtract that number of minutes from the total test time.

When you record the time, write down the altitude, too. Turn the airplane around 180° to heading 90°. Stay on that heading for seven minutes. At the end of that seven-minute interval, record the altitude, VSI reading, time, speed in knots, heading, and engine rpm.

Now it's time for your first turn. Every turn in this benchmark flight will be a 90-degree left turn. Bank far enough so that the attitude of the wings in the turn coordinator looks like the hands of an analog clock set to 8:10. This will be the configuration for every turn.

Begin to come out of the turn at 10° before the desired heading. In the first turn, for example, start coming out at heading 10° so that you'll be straightened out by the time you reach the destination heading of 0°.

After the turn is complete, record the same items: altitude, vertical speed, time, speed in knots, heading, and engine rpm. Repeat this process until the craft stops climbing.

At the end of the test, the jet shows a telltale pattern of reduced vertical speed and altitude and increased airspeed, followed by the reverse (increased vertical speed and altitude and reduced airspeed). When you recognize this pattern, the test is over. Level out the jet, locate the airport, and square back down to the airport at a descent rate of about 500 feet per minute. Land the plane on runway 27R, the same one you took off from.

When you're back on the ground, note when you first began the minute patterns. Add together all the highest altitudes you recorded after noticing the telltale pattern and divide that sum by the number of altitudes recorded in that pattern. The result is an average high altitude that represents the jet's ceiling.

You can perform the same test for the Cessna, but it may take longer, since the Cessna doesn't develop enough speed for the telltale pattern to be easily recognizable. However, it *is* possible. You can also benchmark the aircraft for other factors such as total flight times. While there are limits to every comparison, benchmarking is just one more way to become familiar with what your aircraft can do. And it can be fun, as well.

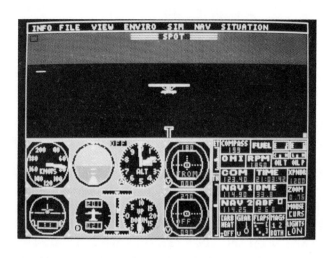

28
Edna's Anniversary

Environment: Summer
Time: 20:55:00
Carb Heat: On
Flaps: Up
Mags: Both
Lights: Off
Aircraft Orientation: On
Auto Coord: On
Sound: On

Winds:

Level 3 Tops	= No winds	
Level 2 Tops	= 6000	
Dir	= 26	
Bot	= 1000	

Speed	= 12	
Turb	= 0	
Level 1 Tops	= 1000	
Dir	= 112	
Bot	= 75	
Speed	= 9	
Turb	= 0	

Surface winds AGL: None

Position Set:

Aircraft North	= 17733.000	
East	= 21543.000	
Alt	= 705.000	
Heading	= 208	

Here it comes down the driveway—a spotless, navy-blue Lincoln Continental carrying Edna Nethery, your passenger for the day. Every year at this time, for the last 15 years, you've been here to take her to her son's home for a summer vacation.

Mrs. Nethery is a wealthy, elderly woman who's used to having things her own way. Her husband was a pilot and he always flew them to their resort home during the summer hiatus. Ever since he passed away, she has been hiring you to fly her once a year on this short, sentimental journey. The weather is clear and unremarkable on this particular afternoon. This may be the easiest $1,000 you'll ever make.

There's only one troublesome thing about this flight: Edna always insists on taking off near dusk and flying into the sunset. That means you'll be landing at your destination—Bradley International Airport—just before dark. Mrs. Nethery is scared of flying in the dark, so you won't have any time to waste on this flight.

You're looking out the windshield at the runway in Southbridge Municipal Airport. This is the airport closest to Sturbridge, Massachusetts, where Mrs. Nethery lives in quiet retirement with a couple of servants and a large assortment of pets. Here's the flight plan:

20:55	**Take off from Southbridge**
20:56	**Tune in Hartford VOR at 114.9**
21:01	**Tune in Brainard NDB at 329**
21:02	**Correct heading to conform to Brainard**
21:03	**Tune in Barnes VOR at 113.0**
21:04	**Tune ADF to 330**
21:06	**Turn 90° right to 330° radial**
21:13	**Turn 90° left to 240° radial**
21:27	**Land at Bradley International**

Visual landmarks are of little importance in this plan, so you'll need to pay close attention to the clock and navigation instruments.

Edna is safely belted in and her chauffeur watches from a safe distance as you perform the preflight checks. It's takeoff time: Throttle up, down the runway, and off we go!

Once in the air, you keep a wary eye on the clock, because you know Edna won't be happy if night falls before you touch down again. The clock now reads 20:56—time to tune in the Hartford, Connecticut, VOR at 114.9.

Hartford is 35–40 miles away at about 236 degrees. You'll want to keep your altitude at about 3000 feet, so your VSI and altimeter become important. You have about three minutes to level the plane off.

It's 21:01. Time to tune the ADF to Brainard at 329. The ADF shows Brainard just a bit west of your present heading. Ease the craft over until Brainard is straight ahead.

At 21:03 you tune in to the Barnes VOR at 113.0 and set the ADF to 330. When the needle centers, you'll make a 90-degree turn right to fly toward Barnes.

About 21:06—the needle has centered and you make the turn.

Now it's time to check the altitude and the VSI again. When everything stabilizes, you remember your passenger. Things have been moving pretty fast up here in the cockpit, and she's been unusually quiet. You look back into the passenger area. There she sits, looking peacefully out the window. Perhaps she's thinking about her late husband, looking forward to seeing her son again, or simply remembering the many times she made this flight in the past.

"Mrs. Nethery," you interrupt.

"Is everything all right?" she replies.

"Yes, ma'am. I just thought you might be ready for your refreshment."

"That sounds like a good idea. I'll have the usual—a Bloody Mary without the Mary."

"Coming right up," you reply, as you retire to the stores to get her a drink. Don't dawdle over the task, though, or you'll overshoot the approach to Bradley, which will become visible when the DME shows that you're 13 or 14 miles from Barnes.

Just in time. Bradley International is out your left window and the flight plan shows that it's time for a left turn. Turn back to a heading of 240° for the final approach. The altitude at Bradley is 174 feet, so you have to lose some altitude. When you're lined up with the runway, put the nose down a bit and prepare to land.

"Fasten your seatbelt, Mrs. Nethery," you remind your passenger.

"Are we there already?" she asks.

"We'll be on the ground in a couple of minutes."

Another year has passed, with one more sentimental flight for Edna Nethery.

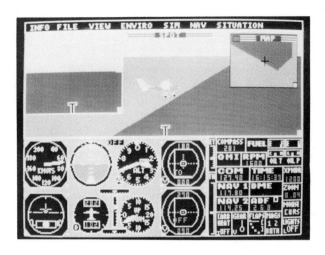

29
Make Mine L.A.

Environment: Spring
Time: 16:12:00
Carb Heat: Off
Flaps: Up
Mags: Both
Lights: Off
Aircraft Orientation: On
Auto Coord: On
Sound: On

Winds:

Level 3 Tops	=	3000
Dir	=	120
Bot	=	2000
Speed	=	5
Turb	=	0
Level 2 Tops	=	2000
Dir	=	125
Bot	=	1000
Speed	=	4
Turb	=	0
Level 1 Tops	=	1000
Dir	=	102
Bot	=	500
Speed	=	3
Turb	=	0

Surface winds AGL:

Depth	=	500
Dir	=	122
Speed	=	2
Turb	=	0

Position Set:

Aircraft North	=	14400.000
East	=	6109.0000
Alt	=	4000.0000
Heading	=	284

I magine yourself a flying physician. Every other month, you charter a plane and fly with your trusty Nurse Fletcher to visit a long list of impoverished patients in Santa Rosalita, Baja California. You don't get paid for this, but do it partly to repay society for the full scholarship you were granted to medical school, and partly because—admit it—you love to fly.

When the adventure starts, you've just finished your semimonthly visit to Santa Rosalita, and are cruising back home toward Los Angeles. You're 4000 feet over Mexico at 4:00 on a Friday afternoon, and you're anxious to get home before dark. First, however, you need to stop at San Diego to refuel your plane and check out the restroom facilities.

It's time to call the tower at San Diego International Airport, also known as Lindbergh Field. Tune in your COM radio to San Diego at 134.8. If there's no answer yet, don't fret. You're still a good distance away. Tune in the Mission Bay VOR at 117.8—it should be well within range. Lindbergh Field is closely in line with Mission Bay from your current position, so it makes sense to adjust your VOR and change course to the new heading.

By the time the San Diego tower responds, you're about 40 miles out, near Ensenada, Baja. The San Diego controllers advise you to take runway 13. That means you'll have to intercept the pattern downwind, passing by the runway and making successive 90-degree turns to get on runway heading.

As you approach San Diego, open up your map display and zoom it all the way out for minimum magnification. San Diego is at the junction of four interstate highways: I-8 from the east, I-15 from the north, I-5 from the northwest, and I-805, the Inland Freeway, from the south. All of them should be clearly visible. Tijuana, Mexico, lies just to the south of here.

Recalibrate your VOR and fly 5°–10° to the east of the indicated heading. In other words, if the VOR says the Mission Bay station is at radial 330, fly instead to the radial at

335–340, because you want to come around the east side of the runway to make your 90-degree turns.

Lindbergh Field is directly in front of I-5. When you see it, lose altitude and level off at about 2000 feet.

You may not be far enough east of the airport to make two 90-degree turns. If not, you'll have to make one large 180-degree turn...which is okay. But if you want to move further east, follow these instructions: Turn to heading 000° and fly by the airport. You'll see two sets of runways, one perpendicular to your position. The other runway is yours. It will be lined up at roughly a 45-degree angle from your approach. Once past the airport—that is, when the runways are out of your view from the cockpit—turn to a heading of 310°, the reciprocal of the runway heading. As you make this turn, you'll fly directly over I-5. If you check your left-rear view, you can see the runway.

Now it's time for those two 90-degree turns. Switch to the rear view. When the runway reaches the middle part of the screen, turn 90°, to 220°.

Check the left view. Just before the runway is straight out that window, turn 90° again, to 130°.

Immediately switch back to the front view and get in line with the runway. If you leveled out at around 2000 feet before, these turns have probably brought you down to about 1100 feet. Lose some more altitude, and coast in for a landing.

These are tricky maneuvers—harder than they sound. If you don't master this landing the first time, try again. Eventually you'll get the hang of it.

While your ship is being serviced, grab a sandwich. But nothing else. You've still got the leg to L.A. to complete, so it's not time to start the weekend yet.

Back in the cockpit, you examine your chart. You've long ago memorized this route, but it never hurts to be sure. Tune in your NAV-1 to the Oceanside VOR at 115.3. You don't want to fly to the indicated radial, but you do want to use it to track. Also tune in the Escondido NDB on the ADF at 374. This will be another aid for tracking.

Take off from runway 13 and start climbing. At about 1500 feet, make a gradual 180-degree turn to the right, steering toward a compass heading of 310°. The angle of this turn should be very shallow, and because the aircraft tends to float out of such a shallow turn, you'll have to periodically compensate. At the end of the turn you should be over the waters of the Pacific Ocean. If not, your turn was too sharp. If this is the case, fly back a bit to about 250°, straighten out, and try the gradual turn again. Once you've established your heading of 310°, continue climbing and level off at 6000 feet.

By the way, things could become very hazardous should you stray off course in this region, because you're flying very close to a large area of restricted military airspace. Just north of San Diego is Miramar Naval Air Station, also known as Fightertown, U.S.A.—the setting for a hit movie of 1986, *Top Gun*. This is where the U.S. Navy sends the cream of its carrier-based fighter pilots for advanced combat training. You certainly don't want to get your single-engine Cessna involved in a dogfight with an F-14 Tomcat.

Glancing out your right window, you can clearly see the Southern California beaches and I-5, which parallels the coastline from San Diego to the City of Angels. Pretty soon you'll be coming up on Oceanside, a small city on the coast. You can tell when you pass it by setting your VOR needle to 90° from your 310° heading—radial 040. When the VOR needle centers, you're passing at 90° from Oceanside, which should come into view directly out the right window.

At this point, tune in to your next VOR station, Santa Catalina Island at 111.4. Use it just as you did Oceanside. You'll fly in the general direction of Catalina for a while, due

to the northwest curvature of the Southern California coastline. Later you'll break northeast, ready to home in on L.A.

So, tune in Santa Catalina and fly toward the VOR heading, but not right at it. The needle will probably center somewhere around 270°; fly to a radial about halfway between 270
and 310.

Before long you'll see Santa Catalina Island from your
front window, preferably just a bit to the left. This is when
you set the VOR needle so it will center at 90° from 285—radial 225. That way, when it centers, you'll be passing 90°
from the Santa Catalina VOR station.

This kind of VOR tracking is an invaluable aid to navigation. Some newer aircraft have an even better system called
RNAV, which in effect allows the pilot to "move" VOR stations all over the map. But you can't have everything.

While you're waiting to pass Catalina, tune in the COM
radio to your home port, Los Angeles International. The frequency is 133.8, and the LAX tower advises you to use runway 07. This means you can intercept the pattern on the base
leg, something you've done many times before.

After passing by Santa Catalina Island, tune in the LAX
VOR at 113.6. You should fly a bit below the indicated radial—turn to about 300°. Why is this? The runway heading is
070°, and the base leg is 90° from the runway heading. That
works out to 340°. To fly below that, take about 30°–45° off
the actual radial, yielding a heading of approximately
295°–310°.

When you tune in LAX just after passing Catalina, the
VOR confirms that it lies at about 340°. Set the needle to center at 070°, the runway heading, and, just before it centers,
turn to that radial. This puts you on your final approach to
LAX. You'll probably be too far away to actually see the airport at this point, but it's there, so hold that radial until the
airstrips come into view.

LAX is a huge airport, and you'll see that there are two distinct sets of runways on this approach. Take your choice, and guide the plane in for a smooth landing.

At last, it's time to relax. Make the most of your weekend in L.A.

30
Dodger in the Sky

Environment: Summer
Time: 15:10:00
Carb Heat: Off
Flaps: Up
Mags: Both
Lights: Off
Aircraft Orientation: On
Auto Coord: On
Sound: On

Winds:
Level 3 Tops	=	8000
Dir	=	185
Bot	=	7000
Speed	=	4
Turb	=	0
Level 2 Tops	=	6790
Dir	=	145
Bot	=	5000
Speed	=	5
Turb	=	0
Level 1 Tops	=	4600

Dir	=	129
Bot	=	1467
Speed	=	8
Turb	=	0

Surface winds AGL:
Depth	=	1000
Dir	=	155
Speed	=	4
Turb	=	0

Position Set:
Aircraft North	=	15247.000
East	=	5553.0000
Alt	=	9616.0000
Heading	=	229

Clouds:
Level 1 Tops	=	6000
Base	=	1500
Level 2 Tops	=	10000
Base	=	7000
Ground Fog	=	None

125

Sunny days *aren't* here again—it's time for another of the "unfair"-weather adventures. And over the ocean, no less.

This adventure begins in midair, 9600 feet above the Pacific. You had set out for a nice flight from San Diego to Van Nuys, but a summer storm moved in much more quickly than had been predicted. Now you're flying blind in a thick layer of clouds, and you'll have to depend on instruments to guide you to your destination.

First things first—make sure your plane is leveled off and stabilized; then tune your NAV-1 radio to the Los Angeles VOR at 113.6. The plan is to fly toward Los Angeles, then make the turn to nearby Van Nuys. Adjust your VOR TO needle and turn to the new heading—probably somewhere around 037°, a sharp turn from your initial course of 229°. While making the turn, be careful to watch that artificial horizon. It's easy to flip the plane over and lose control when there's no scenery visible to help you orient yourself.

After the turn is complete and everything is stabilized again, call Van Nuys at 118.45 on your COM radio to see which runway you should use. Hmmm...no answer. You're probably too far away. But you're still getting a strong signal from the L.A. VOR, so stick to this course and hope that the Van Nuys tower will come into range before too long. In the meantime, pay close attention to that VOR needle and make any minor corrections that are necessary to stay on course. Maintain your altitude as well. When you're flying blind, you can't take any chances.

To bring another instrument into play, switch on your automatic direction finder (ADF). When the ADF dial appears, tune in the Compton NDB at 378 on the ADF radio. If you're on course to L.A., you should notice that you're flying almost directly toward Compton, too. As always, you can measure your progress with the plane's distance-measuring equipment (DME). It should confirm that you're closing on the L.A. VOR.

Every few miles, keep checking your COM radio for the Van Nuys tower. (You can't just leave the COM radio tuned to

118.45 and expect the report to appear when you come within range; you must periodically tune to a slightly different frequency, then retune to 118.45.) Before long, Van Nuys will crackle into earshot with a report similar to this:

Van Nuys Information Whisky 22:00 Zulu weather—measured ceiling 1400 overcast—visibility 10—temperature 80—wind 155 at 4—altimeter 29.95—landing and departing runway 16—ILS runway 16R instrument approach in use. Localizer frequency 111.30—advise controller on initial airport contact you have Whisky...

Reassured, you now know *exactly* where you're headed—runway 16R. These winds could present a problem, though. You may have to crab and re-adjust the VOR and your heading every five miles or so.

Stay on course toward L.A. until the DME shows that you're about five miles out. At that point, switch your NAV-1 radio from Los Angeles to the Van Nuys VOR at 113.1—but don't change course quite yet. Instead, set the VOR needle at 300° and wait until it centers. You're doing this because you have to intercept the pattern on the downwind. Eventually you're going to fly along the east side of the Van Nuys airport (to the right of it, from your point of view) on a heading of 340°, the reciprocal of the runway heading. A final U-turn to 160° will then line you up with runway 16R.

In the meantime, while you're waiting for that VOR needle to center at 300, descend to about 5000 feet. You might see some kind of horizon between 6000 and 7000 feet, but even this meager view quickly disappears as you pass into yet another layer of clouds. At least you'll be in better position for your final descent at Van Nuys.

As soon as the VOR needle centers at 300, change course to 300°. Again, pay close attention to the artificial horizon to avoid throwing the plane into an unwelcome barrel roll.

When the plane is leveled out and stabilized at 300°, immediately make another turn to 340°. With any luck, this should put you on the reciprocal of the runway heading just east of the airport. Now you're in the pattern, even though you're still 15 miles or so from Van Nuys.

On the way there, you recall that your favorite baseball team, the Los Angeles Dodgers, is playing a home game today. You're just about over Dodger Stadium, and for a fleeting moment you consider buzzing the ballpark for a close-up peek. Then you come to your senses. With these clouds, you'd be forced to fly practically at bleacher level for a worthwhile view. Too dangerous—and you're too much of a Dodger fan to risk a premature promotion to Angel.

The DME should indicate how far you are from Van Nuys. When you're flying on instruments, though, it's always advisable to use as many instruments as possible, so try using the VOR again to determine your angle. Keeping it tuned to Van Nuys at 113.1, set the needle at 250°. When it centers, you'll know that you are passing Van Nuys.

Watch the DME when the VOR needle centers. It should hardly be changing. That's because the airport should be directly to your left, and you're passing nearby. If the DME reads 7 or more, you've got plenty of room to maneuver. If it's less than 7, be careful. You may be too close. Either start over, or cut every turn described from now on just a little sharper, to compensate.

Once past Van Nuys (the VOR needle drifts left of center), re-adjust the VOR needle to 200°. Stick to your current heading of 340°. When the needle centers again, you'll be in good shape for a left turn to 250°, the base leg.

After you've turned to 250°, it's time to start landing procedures. Lose some altitude and speed, and get ready for your turn to final. Set the VOR to 160°, the runway heading for 16R. Just before the needle centers, turn to 160°.

If you're a little off—that is, if the needle starts to move after your turn—center it and fly to the indicated heading. If